THE CONRAN COOKBOOKS

PASTA PERFECT

ANNA DEL CONTE

CONRAN OCTOPUS

This edition published in 1991 by
Conran Octopus Limited
37 Shelton Street
London WC2H 9HN

First published in 1986

Photographer Paul Bussell
Editorial Consultant Caro Hobhouse
House Editor Susie Ward
Art Director Douglas Wilson
Art Editor Clive Hayball
Photographic Art Direction Valerie Wright Heneghan
Home Economist Lisa Collard
Photographic Stylist Sue Russel-Fell
Art Assistant Nina Thomas

ISBN 1 85029 355 4

The publishers would like to thank the following
for their assistance with photographic props:
Heal's, 196 Tottenham Court Road, London W1;
The Conran Shop, Fulham Road, London SW3;
Habitat Designs Limited

Title page: Pasta with Mixed Vegetables (page 34/35)

Typeset by SX Composing, Essex
Printed and bound in China

CONTENTS

INTRODUCTION

There is no food that is so versatile, and yet so simple, as pasta. It consists of nothing but flour and water or flour and eggs, yet it can be served in a thousand and one ways. Pasta can play host to almost every flavour you can imagine, providing healthy nourishment in a variety of delicious ways quite unmatched by any other foodstuff.

Types of pasta

Factory-made *dried pasta* – of which the most common kinds are spaghetti, noodles of various kinds, shapes such as fusilli, conchiglie and farfalle, lasagne and the soup pastas – is made from durum wheat ground into semolina and mixed to a paste with water. The dough is forced through perforated metal plates to form the appropriate shape of pasta and then dried. It should be buff-yellow, translucent and slightly shiny.

The '*fresh pasta*' sold in specialist shops or supermarkets is made with durum wheat semolina, flour, eggs and water, and while convenient, is certainly not as good as homemade pasta, and is actually often not any better tasting than good dried pasta.

Homemade pasta has a lightness and delicacy that neither shop-bought 'fresh pasta' nor dried pasta can match. So, when you want to make a recipe which calls for fresh pasta do try to make it yourself, either by hand or with the help of a machine. It is not easy to make pasta by hand without practice, lots of time and, most difficult of all, a long thin pasta rolling-pin.

Luckily there are good machines available to speed-up the task. The electric machines make an excellent pasta, but they are expensive, noisy and difficult to clean. The hand-cranked machines are cheap and easily obtained.

COOKING TIMES FOR PASTA

Cooking time is calculated after the water returns to the boil

Homemade pasta	Fresh	Dried
tagliatelle	30 seconds-1 minute	1-2 minutes
tonnarelli	1 minute	1½-2 minutes
lasagne	15 seconds	45 seconds
stuffed shapes	5-6 minutes	7-9 minutes

Shop bought fresh pasta usually takes a little longer.

Dried pasta	
vermicelli	1½-3 minutes
spaghettini	6-7 minutes
linguine	7-9 minutes
spaghetti, bigoli or long macaroni or bucatini	7-9 minutes
tagliatelle	10-12 minutes
farfalle	8-10 minutes
conchigliette or small tubular shapes	7-9 minutes
gnocchi, ditali, orecchiette, conchiglie or medium tubular shapes	9-11 minutes
penne rigatoni or large tubular shapes	9-12 minutes

Cooking pasta

It is easy to cook pasta, but it can be ruined by carelessness. We say in Italian, 'Gli spaghetti amano la compagnia' ('spaghetti loves company') – you should never leave the kitchen while the pasta is in the pot. Timing is crucial.

Pasta needs to be cooked in a large pot and a lot of water – at least 1¾ pints (1 litre) to 3½ oz (100 g) pasta – and for the recipes in this book you will need a lidded saucepan holding at least 7 pints (4 litres). Bring the water to the boil, and then add about 1½ tablespoons cooking salt. Slide all the pasta into the boiling water, stir with a wooden fork or spoon to separate the pasta shapes and cover, so that the water returns to the boil as soon as possible. Remove the lid and adjust the heat so that the water boils briskly, but does not boil over. Start the timing from the exact moment at which the pasta comes back to the boil.

Sauces for different pasta shapes

Although I have given suggestions for types and shapes of pasta within the recipes for this book, they do not all need to be followed slavishly. There are, however, certain basic rules which govern the choice of sauce to serve with the different types and shapes of pastas. In general, long thin shapes should be dressed with a light, olive oil-based sauce which allows the strands to remain slippery and separate. Thicker long shapes like bucatini and ziti are happiest with heavier sauces containing meat, or based on cream, cheese and eggs. Ditali and the other medium-size tubular pasta are perfect with vegetables of any kind, and are also good for pasta salads. Large short pasta, like macaroni and penne, are marvellous for rich meat sauces or ragùs, or for baked dishes.

Draining pasta

Pasta should be drained as soon as it is *al dente* (literally, 'to the tooth'), which means that you must be able to feel its texture when you bite into it. However, if the pasta is going to be cooked further, by baking or frying, drain it when still slightly undercooked. Pasta for salads should also be especially al dente.

Draining pasta properly is important. Use a colander large enough to contain all the pasta you have cooked. Tip in the pasta, give the colander 2 sharp shakes and immediately turn the pasta into a heated bowl or dish, or into the frying pan with the sauce. Pasta should never be overdrained as it needs to be slippery for coating with the sauce. It should be dressed as soon as it is drained.

Quantities of pasta for each serving

The recipes in this book are nearly all for 4 normal helpings of pasta, but people's appetites vary tremendously. As a guide, I find 3 oz (85 g) sufficient for a normal helping (but I cook twice as much for my two sons!). I am often asked if my quantities are for first or main courses, but in fact I find it makes surprisingly little difference, and that people eat the same amount whether there is a main course of meat or fish, or just a salad, to follow.

Anna Del Conte

HOME MADE PASTA

You should allow at least 2 hours for the whole process.

————— FOR A NORMAL SERVING FOR 3 PEOPLE —————

2 medium eggs
7 oz (200 g) plain strong flour

Put the flour on a work surface, make a well in the centre and crack in the eggs. (For green pasta add 5 oz (140 g) cooked spinach at this point.) Using a fork or your fingers, break up the eggs, gradually drawing in the flour. When the mixture thickens, work quickly together to form a ball of dough. Scrape the work surface clean, dust lightly with flour and wash your hands.

Alternatively, the dough may be made in a food processor. Put the flour into the goblet, switch on the machine and drop the eggs through the funnel. Process until the flour and eggs form a ball of dough. Turn the dough on to the lightly floured work surface.

Knead the dough, occasionally slapping it hard against the work surface, for at least 6 minutes. (This is very important for the texture of the pasta.) Wrap the dough in clingfilm and set aside to rest for at least 30 minutes or up to 3-4 hours.

Unwrap the dough and lightly dust the work surface with flour. Knead the dough as before for a further 2 minutes, then divide it into 4 equal parts. Take one piece of dough and re-wrap the remainder in clingfilm and place them in a bowl, covering it with a cloth.

Set the rollers of the machine at the widest opening. Flatten the piece of dough slightly and run it through the machine 5 or 6 times, folding the sheet over and giving it a 180° turn each time. When the dough is smooth, run the sheet, unfolded, through all the settings, closing the rollers one notch at a time until you achieve the desired thickness. If the sheet tears or sticks to the machine, dust it on both sides with flour. For tonnarelli (square spaghetti) stop the rolling-out at the second from last setting. For tagliatelle or tagliolini stop at the last but one. For flat sheet pasta stop at the last setting.

(However, I have found that if the atmosphere is very damp, dough rolled out too thinly cannot be stuffed for tortelli or other small shapes as, instead of drying, it becomes more and more soggy when filled with the stuffing. If you find this happening, stop rolling out at the last but one setting.) Roll out the dough to the last setting only for lasagne or cannelloni.

Long pasta Lay each pasta sheet on a clean tea towel, letting about one third of its length hang down over the edge of the work surface. Leave until the pasta is dry to the touch and slightly leathery, although still pliable. This process takes about 30 minutes, depending on the humidity of the atmosphere and the texture of the pasta, and is essential to prevent the noodles from sticking together. Feed each sheet through the broad cutters of the machine for tagliatelle or fettuccine, or through the narrow ones for tonnarelli or tagliolini.

Separate the cut noodles and spread them out on clean tea towels, lightly dusted with flour or semolina. The noodles are now ready to be cooked, or they can be dried and then stored in an airtight tin or plastic bag. Dried homepasta is very brittle and breaks easily.

Lasagne and cannelloni Cut each pasta sheet into squares about 5×3½ in (12×8.5 cm) for lasagne or 4×3 in (10×7.5 cm) for cannelloni. (You can cook them straight away or leave to dry as for long pasta.)

Small stuffed pasta shapes You must work while the pasta is still fresh and pliable. Stuff the pasta sheets, one or two at a time, depending on the shape being made. Keep the remainder wrapped in clingfilm.

Cook them straight away or leave them until the next day, spread apart on a clean cloth, dusted with flour.

The various types of (dried) pasta used in this book:
1. Vermicelli 2. Green Tagliatelle 3. White Tagliatelle 4. Cannelloni 5. Lasagnette 6. White Lasagne 7. Green Lasagne 8. Tonnarelli 9. Paglia e Fieno 10. Farfalle 11. Pipette Rigate 12. Ruote 13. Ravioli 14. Green Fusilli 15. White Fusilli 16. Conchiglie 17. Conchigliette 18. Macaroni 19. Rigatoni 20 Ditali 21. Ditalini 22. Gnocchi 23. Orecchiette 24. Green and White Penne 25. Ziti 26. Bucatini 27. Linguine 28. Wholewheat Spaghetti 29. Spaghettini 30. Lumache

FETTUCCINE WITH PESTO

This exquisite sauce is traditionally served with trenette, the Genoese name for a kind of wide linguine. But pesto is also good with fettucine or pappardelle and it goes well with long wholewheat pasta. If you cannot find good pecorino romano, use Parmesan only. I want to emphasize yet again how important good cheese is for these pasta sauces. Remember that ready-grated Parmesan sold in cartons bears no relation to the real Parmesan.

—————————— SERVES 4 ——————————

fettuccine made with 3 eggs and 11 oz (300 g) strong flour (page 6); or 1 lb (450 g) shop-bought fresh fettuccine; or 12 oz (340 g) dried egg fettuccine or tagliatelle
2 tablespoons pine nuts
2 oz (50 g) basil leaves
2 cloves garlic, peeled
4 fl oz (110 ml) extra virgin olive oil
salt and freshly ground black pepper
2 oz (50 g) freshly grated Parmesan cheese
2 tablespoons freshly grated pecorino romano cheese

Toast the pine nuts for about 10 minutes in a low oven 250°F (120°C, gas mark ½).

Combine the basil, garlic, pine nuts, oil, salt and pepper in a blender or food processor and process at high speed until evenly blended. Turn the mixture into a heated serving bowl and stir in the cheeses. Check the seasoning.

Meanwhile, cook the pasta in plenty of boiling salted water. Drain, reserving 2 or 3 tablespoons of the cooking water. Immediately turn the pasta into the bowl with the pesto, add the reserved cooking water, toss well and serve immediately.

FETTUCCINE WITH HERBS AND NUTS

Illustrated on page 11

This sauce, made with uncooked herbs and nuts, has a distinctive, fresh taste. Do be sure to buy fresh walnuts. Buy them from a supplier who has a quick turnover. Old walnuts have a rancid taste so penetrating that even one stale nut can ruin a dish. A good sauce also for wholewheat spaghetti.

—————————— SERVES 4 ——————————

12 oz (340 g) fettuccine, trenette or wholewheat spaghetti
1 oz (25 g) pine nuts
2 tablespoons chopped parsley
2 tablespoons chopped fresh marjoram
1 oz (25 g) shelled walnuts
1 clove garlic, peeled
salt and freshly ground black pepper
5 tablespoons olive oil
4 tablespoons freshly grated pecorino or Parmesan cheese
for the garnish
2 sticks celery, with the threads removed, cut into matchstick strips

Spread the pine nuts out on a baking tray and toast for 10 minutes in a low oven 250°F (220°C, gas mark ½). Meanwhile, bring a large saucepan of salted water to the boil.

Put the pine nuts, parsley, marjoram, walnuts, garlic, salt and plenty of pepper into a blender or food processor and process for 15 seconds. Gradually add the oil and blend for a few seconds, pushing the mixture down occasionally with a spatula. Check the seasoning.

Transfer the mixture to an ovenproof serving bowl and place in a very low oven 225°F (110°C, gas mark ¼).

Cook the pasta in salted boiling water. Drain, reserving 2 tablespoons of the cooking water, then immediately turn the pasta into the bowl with the herb mixture and add the reserved water. Toss, add the grated cheese and toss again until the pasta is well coated. Sprinkle the celery on top and serve as quickly as possible.

Above: Fettuccine with Pesto

SPAGHETTI WITH SAFFRON

*One day, when I planned ossobuchi for dinner, I realized
that I did not have any Italian rice for the risotto alla
milanese to accompany them. I used spaghetti instead
and the dish was a great success. It can of course also
be served with other meat dishes, or in its own right.
I prefer to use Italian saffron powder, which is
sweeter and more aromatic than saffron strands. If you
use the strands, fry them in a dry heavy pan, preferably
cast-iron, for 30 seconds or so until they become
darker. Then crumble them. The frying makes the
saffron more aromatic.*

SERVES 4

10 oz (275 g) spaghetti
2 oz (50 g) butter
1 shallot, very finely chopped
⅓ teaspoon saffron powder or saffron strands
4 fl oz (110 ml) dry white wine
4 tablespoons double cream
salt and freshly ground black pepper
1⅓ teaspoons turmeric
for the garnish
a large bunch of parsley, finely chopped

Put half the butter in a small saucepan. Add the shallot
and sauté gently until soft and transparent, but not
brown.

Meanwhile, heat the saffron strands, if used, in a dry
cast-iron pan. Crumble the strands.

Dissolve the crumbled saffron strands or the saffron
powder in 4 tablespoons of boiling water.

Add the wine to the pan with the shallot and simmer
for 5 minutes, then stir in the dissolved saffron. Cook
very gently for 10 minutes. Blend in the cream and bring
slowly to the boil, stirring constantly. Allow to boil for 1
minute. Taste and check seasonings.

Meanwhile, cook the spaghetti in plenty of boiling
salted water with the turmeric. Drain, then immediately
return the spaghetti to the pan in which it was cooked.

Toss immediately with the remaining butter and then
with the saffron sauce.

Transfer the spaghetti to a large heated serving dish
and sprinkle with the parsley. Surround with the ossobuchi and serve immediately.

TAGLIATELLE WITH POPPY SEEDS
Illustrated on page 12

*This sauce originated in the regions of Italy which at one
time formed part of the Austro-Hungarian Empire, and
shows all the influences of Central European cuisine.
The poppy seeds and cumin combine beautifully with
pasta. The dish can be served on its own as a first
course for 4 or as an accompaniment to roast lamb,
served simply in its own cooking juices, in which case it
will serve 6.*

SERVES 4

tagliatelle made with 3 eggs and 11 oz (300 g) strong flour (page
6); or 1 lb (450 g) shop-bought fresh tagliatelle; or
12 oz (340 g) dried egg tagliatelle
2 tablespoons poppy seeds
1 teaspoon cumin seeds
3 oz (85 g) butter
salt

Put the poppy and cumin seeds into a mortar and pound
together with a pestle, or pound with a rolling pin on a
wooden board.

Melt the butter in a small saucepan and, as soon as it
begins to foam, stir in the ground seeds. Cook for 20
seconds, then turn off the heat.

Meanwhile, cook the tagliatelle in plenty of boiling
salted water. Drain, then immediately turn into a heated
serving bowl. Pour over the butter and seed mixture
and toss well. Serve immediately.

Top: Fettuccine with Herbs and Nuts (page 8), below: Spaghetti with Saffron.

Top: Tagliatelle with Poppy Seeds (page 10). Below: Spaghetti in Tomato Sauce with Cinnamon and Bay Leaves.

SPAGHETTI IN TOMATO SAUCE WITH CINNAMON AND BAY LEAVES

This is a recipe from the past, when spices and herbs were used more liberally than today, although during the last decade they have made a long-awaited come-back. This sauce is proof of their excellent value in cooking.

———————— SERVES 4 ————————

12 oz (340 g) spaghetti
4 tablespoons olive oil
1 large onion, finely chopped
2 lb (900 g) fresh ripe tomatoes, skinned and chopped, or 1 lb 5 oz (600 g) tinned chopped tomatoes
10 fresh bay leaves
¼ teaspoon ground cinnamon
salt and freshly ground black pepper

Heat the oil in a large heavy frying pan, add the onion and sauté until transparent. Add the tomatoes, the bay leaves, cinnamon, salt and a generous grinding of pepper. Cook, uncovered, for 15 minutes over a moderate heat, stirring occasionally.

Meanwhile, cook the spaghetti in plenty of boiling salted water. Drain, then immediately turn the spaghetti into the frying pan. Stir-fry for about 1 minute. Serve immediately.

FUSILLI WITH FRESH HERBS AND GARLIC

Illustrated on page 15

The excellence of this simple sauce relies mainly on the ingredients and the way they are treated. Use fresh herbs, not dried, and extra virgin olive oil. The herbs should be chopped by hand rather than in a food processor.
This dish is a good accompaniment to baked or grilled fish, in which case the quantities given here are enough for 6 persons.

———————— SERVES 4 ————————

12 oz (340 g) dried fusilli; or 1 lb shop-bought fresh fusilli
1 oz (25 g) parsley
1 oz (25 g) basil
1 tablespoon marjoram
1 tablespoon thyme
½ tablespoon wild fennel or fennel tops
1 tablespoon sage
½ tablespoon rosemary
1-2 cloves garlic, peeled
salt and freshly ground black pepper
6 tablespoons extra virgin olive oil

Chop all the herbs and the garlic together. Put them into a small bowl, add salt and pepper to taste and about half the oil. Mix well, then leave to stand for at least 30 minutes.

Cook the fusilli in plenty of boiling salted water.

Meanwhile, put the remaining oil and the herb mixture into a large heavy frying pan. Sauté for 1 minute, then remove from the heat.

Drain the pasta, then immediately turn it into the pan. Return the pan to a moderate heat and stir-fry for about 1 minute until the pasta is well coated with the sauce. Serve immediately, either straight from the pan, or transfer to a heated serving dish.

13

SPAGHETTINI WITH GARLIC, OIL AND CHILLI

This very popular and extremely quick sauce is made throughout central Italy. It is very tasty, requiring a very fruity olive oil.

―――――― SERVES 4 ――――――

12 oz (340 g) spaghettini or spaghetti
5 tablespoons extra virgin olive oil
3 cloves garlic, peeled and sliced
1 dried chilli, seeded and crumbled
salt

Cook the pasta in plenty of boiling salted water.

Meanwhile, heat the oil, garlic and chilli in a large heavy frying pan. Sauté for 1 minute. Be careful not to burn the garlic.

Drain the spaghetti, then immediately turn it into the frying pan. Stir-fry for about 1 minute, then serve immediately.

PASTA WITH FRIED EGGS

This has always been one of my family's favourite supper dishes. It is as simple as it is deliciously satisfying. The eggs should be eaten mixed in with the pasta. If you cannot find good pecorino, use Parmesan or mature farmhouse Cheddar.

―――――― SERVES 4 ――――――

12 oz (340 g) ziti or bucatini
4 tablespoons olive oil
3 cloves garlic, peeled and bruised
½-1 dried chilli, seeded and crumbled
4 eggs
salt
2 oz (50 g) pecorino romano cheese, freshly grated

Heat half the oil with the garlic and chilli in a large frying pan and sauté until the garlic is coloured but not brown. Remove and discard the garlic.

Break the eggs carefully into the pan and cook over a low heat until the whites are set. Sprinkle the whites only with salt (not the yolks, or they will harden).

Meanwhile, cook the pasta in plenty of boiling salted water. Drain, then immediately add the remaining oil to the pasta and toss well. Mix in the pecorino.

Divide the pasta into 4 portions and put each portion on to a heated individual plate. Place a fried egg on top of each portion and serve immediately.

Clockwise, from top left: Fusilli with Fresh Herbs and Garlic (page 13); Pasta (in this case, ziti) with Fried Eggs; Spaghettini with Garlic, Oil and Chilli.

Below: Tonnarelli with Mushrooms, Spices and Marjoram, top: Ziti with Sultanas, Almonds and Breadcrumbs.

TONNARELLI WITH MUSHROOMS SPICES AND MARJORAM

I had this dish in Montello in Veneto. The heavenly sauce was made only with porcini (ceps), which are, alas, hard to find in this country. Adding a few dried porcini greatly improves the bland taste of cultivated mushrooms.

――――― SERVES 4 ―――――

tonnarelli made with 3 eggs and 11 oz (300 g) strong flour (page 6);
or 1 lb (450 g) shop-bought fresh spaghetti; or 12 oz (340 g) dried
egg tagliatelle
¾ oz (20 g) dried porcini (wild mushrooms)
3 oz (85 g) butter
1 tablespoon olive oil
1 clove garlic, peeled and bruised
8 oz (225 g) cultivated flat mushrooms or oyster mushrooms, sliced
a pinch of ground cinnamon
a pinch of grated nutmeg
salt and freshly ground black pepper
1 tablespoon chopped fresh marjoram or 2 teaspoons dried
marjoram
4 tablespoons freshly grated Parmesan cheese
for serving
extra grated Parmesan cheese

Put the porcini into a cupful of warm water and leave to soak for 30 minutes. Remove them carefully, reserving the soaking liquid, rinse them under cold running water, dry thoroughly and cut them into small pieces.

Strain the soaking liquid through a sieve lined with muslin or kitchen paper and reserve.

Heat 2 oz (50 g) of the butter, the oil and garlic in a frying pan until the garlic begins to colour, then discard it. Add the porcini and sauté gently for 5 minutes.

Add the sliced mushrooms. Sauté over a moderate heat until the mushrooms have absorbed all the fat. Sprinkle with the cinnamon, nutmeg, salt and pepper, and reduce the heat to low. Cook for a further 10 minutes. If the sauce becomes too dry, add a couple of tablespoons of the reserved soaking liquid. Mix in the marjoram. Check the seasoning.

Meanwhile, cook the tonnarelli in plenty of boiling salted water. Drain, reserving half a cupful of the cooking water, then immediately turn the tonnarelli into a heated serving bowl and mix in the remaining butter and grated Parmesan. Spoon over the mushroom sauce and toss very well. If the pasta seems too dry, add a little of the reserved cooking water and mix well. Serve immediately with extra grated Parmesan.

ZITI WITH SULTANAS, ALMONDS AND BREADCRUMBS

The mixture may seem odd, but do try this delectable yet easy sauce from southern Italy.

――――― SERVES 4 ―――――

12 oz (340 g) ziti or long macaroni
2 oz (50 g) sultanas
6 tablespoons olive oil
4 oz (120 g) fresh white breadcrumbs
2 oz (50 g) blanched almonds, chopped
salt and freshly ground black pepper
8 fresh basil leaves, shredded, or 2 tablespoons chopped parsley

Put the sultanas into a cupful of warm water and leave to soak for about 15 minutes. Drain and dry thoroughly on kitchen paper.

Heat the oil in a saucepan, then stir in the breadcrumbs. As soon as all the oil has been absorbed, mix in the sultanas and the almonds. Season to taste with salt and plenty of pepper. Stir-fry for 2 minutes.

Meanwhile, cook the macaroni in plenty of boiling salted water. Drain, then turn the macaroni into a heated serving bowl. Pour over the sauce, toss, decorate with the basil leaves or parsley, and serve immediately.

TONNARELLI IN GORGONZOLA SAUCE

For this delectable sauce you need real Gorgonzola;
Dolcelatte will not do as a substitute.

──────── SERVES 4 ────────

tonnarelli made with 3 eggs and 11 oz (300 g) strong flour (page 6);
or 1 lb (450 g) shop-bought fresh tagliatelle or spaghetti; or 12 oz
(340 g) dried egg tagliatelle
2 tablespoons shelled pistachio nuts
a little milk
2 oz (50 g) butter
4 oz (110 g) Gorgonzola cheese
5 fl oz (150 ml) single cream
2 tablespoons brandy
salt and freshly ground black pepper

Plunge the pistachios into boiling water for just 20
seconds, then drain and remove the skins. Put the
skinned pistachios into a small bowl and cover with a
little milk.

Put the butter and Gorgonzola into a heavy saucepan.
Cook over the gentlest heat until melted, stirring constantly. Add the cream and brandy and cook for a further
5 minutes, stirring frequently.

Meanwhile, drain the pistachios and chop very finely.

Remove the sauce from the heat, stir in the pistachios and season with plenty of pepper and salt if
necessary. Spoon into a heated serving dish.

Keep warm in a low oven 250°F (120°C, gas mark ½).

Cook the tonnarelli in plenty of boiling salted water.
Drain, reserving a cupful of the cooking water, then
immediately turn the tonnarelli into the dish with the
Gorgonzola sauce. Toss thoroughly. If the dish seems
too dry, add a few tablespoons of the reserved cooking
water and mix well. Serve immediately.

Clockwise, from top: Spaghetti with Pecorino and Peppercorns (page 22); Tonnarelli in Gorgonzola sauce; Penne with Four Cheeses (page 22).

Left: Fettuccine with Cream and Butter, right: Green Tagliatelle with Lemon and Cream.

GREEN TAGLIATELLE WITH LEMON AND CREAM

This delicate pasta dish is ideal as an accompaniment to meat, and it will serve 6 in this way. I can recommend it with Wiener Schnitzel or with breaded pork chops. Of course, like all pasta, it is also perfect served in the true Italian way, on its own as a first course, in which case it will serve 4. Egg tagliatelle may also be used.

--- SERVES 6 ---

green tagliatelle made with 2 eggs and 7 oz (200 g) strong flour and
5 oz (140 g) cooked spinach (page 6); or 1 lb (450 g) shop-bought
fresh green tagliatelle; or 12 oz (340 g) dried green tagliatelle
1 oz (25 g) butter
4-5 fresh sage leaves, or 3 dried sage leaves
5 tablespoons lemon juice
7 fl oz (200 ml) single cream
salt and freshly ground white pepper
2 oz (50 g) freshly grated Parmesan cheese

Put the butter with the sage into a small heavy saucepan and heat gently until melted. Add the lemon juice and stir over a moderate heat for 30 seconds.

Reduce the heat and add the cream to the pan. Cook, stirring constantly, until just below boiling point. Add salt to taste and a very generous amount of pepper. Cover and keep warm on the corner of the cooker, or over a large saucepan of hot water.

Cook the tagliatelle in plenty of boiling salted water. Drain, reserving one cupful of the cooking water, and immediately turn into a heated serving dish. Dress with a few tablespoons of sauce and a sprinkling of the Parmesan. Toss well, mix in the remaining sauce, and, if the dish seems too dry, add a couple of tablespoons of the reserved cooking water and mix well. Serve immediately, handing the remaining Parmesan separately in a bowl.

FETTUCCINE WITH CREAM AND BUTTER

This recipe is now famous everywhere, better known as fettuccine 'all' Alfredo', after the Roman restaurateur who used to give each serving of pasta a final toss with his gold fork and spoon. I find that the sauce is infinitely better with crème fraîche. You can make your own by mixing together equal amounts of double and sour cream and leaving it covered, at room temperature, for about 8 to 10 hours, until thickened. Place in the refrigerator and use within 5 days. This sauce is excellent also with fresh or dried tortellini.

--- SERVES 4 ---

fettuccine made with 3 eggs and 11 oz (300 g) strong flour (page 6);
or 1 lb (450 g) shop-bought fresh fettuccine or tagliatelle; or 12 oz
(340 g) dried egg tagliatelle
7 fl oz (200 ml) double cream or crème fraîche
1 oz (25 g) butter
salt and freshly ground white pepper
2 oz (50 g) Parmesan cheese, freshly grated
for serving (optional)
extra grated Parmesan cheese

Heat half the cream with the butter in a large, heavy frying pan. Simmer gently for about 1 minute.

Meanwhile, cook the pasta in plenty of boiling salted water. Drain, reserving half a cupful of the cooking water, then immediately turn the pasta into the frying pan. Toss over a low heat for a few seconds. Add salt and pepper to taste, then mix in the remaining cream, the Parmesan and 4-5 tablespoons of the reserved cooking water.

Toss until the pasta is evenly coated with the sauce then serve immediately, direct from the pan, accompanied by extra grated Parmesan in a bowl, if liked.

PENNE WITH FOUR CHEESES
Illustrated on pages 18/19

Parmesan and Gruyère cheese are always included in this sauce, but other good melting cheeses such as Jarlsberg, Edam or Lancashire, may be substituted for Bel Paese or Fontina.

──────── SERVES 4 ────────

12 oz (340 g) penne or macaroni
2 oz (50 g) butter
4 tablespoons double cream
2 oz (50 g) Gruyère cheese, cut into small slivers
2 oz (50 g) Bel Paese cheese, cut into small slivers
2 oz (50 g) Italian Fontina cheese, cut into small slivers
1 oz (25 g) Parmesan cheese, freshly grated
salt and freshly ground black pepper

Heat the oven to 425°F (220°C, gas mark 7).
   Cook pasta in plenty of boiling salted water. Drain, then immediately turn the pasta into a heated ovenproof serving dish. Immediately add the butter and cream and toss well, then add all the cheeses, salt and plenty of pepper. Mix thoroughly and put the dish in the oven for 5 minutes, just long enough for all the cheeses to melt. Serve immediately.

SPAGHETTI WITH PECORINO AND PEPPERCORNS
Illustrated on pages 18/19

If you like pure, unadulterated flavours this old Roman dish will appeal to you. You will need good-quality thin spaghetti and excellent pecorino romano, a cheese which you can buy from Italian specialist shops. It should be whitish and compact in appearance, with a piquant, salty flavour, without that sickly taste which means the cheese is too old or of poor quality. The addition of the green peppercorns is my own idea, which I find works very well.

──────── SERVES 4 ────────

12 oz (340 g) thin spaghetti or wholewheat spaghetti
4 oz (120 g) pecorino romano cheese
salt and freshly ground black pepper
1 tablespoon green peppercorns, lightly bruised
for the garnish
1 oz (25 g) fresh basil leaves, torn into small pieces

Cook the spaghetti in plenty of boiling salted water.
   Meanwhile, grate the pecorino and put it into an ovenproof serving bowl. Add a great deal of black pepper and the green peppercorns. Add a couple of tablespoons of the cooking water and mix thoroughly. Put the bowl into a very low oven 225°F (110°C, gas mark ¼).
   Drain the spaghetti, reserving a cupful of the cooking water. Immediately turn the spaghetti into the bowl with the pecorino and toss well. If the dish seems too dry, add a little of the reserved cooking water and mix thoroughly.
   Sprinkle the basil on top and serve immediately.

FUSILLI WITH TOMATO AND MOZZARELLA SAUCE

Illustrated on page 33

This sauce must be made with fresh tomatoes, cooked for a very short time to retain their full flavour. Make it when local tomatoes are in season.

───────── SERVES 4 ─────────

12 oz (340 g) fusilli, green, white or mixed
1½ lb (675 g) fresh ripe tomatoes, skinned, seeded and roughly chopped
2 cloves garlic, peeled and finely sliced
4 tablespoons olive oil
1 Italian mozzarella cheese, coarsely grated
2 oz (50 g) pecorino romano or Parmesan cheese, freshly grated
1 tablespoon oregano
salt and freshly ground black pepper

Heat the oven to 425°F (220°C, gas mark 7).

Put the tomatoes, garlic and oil into a heavy saucepan and cook over a moderate heat for 5 minutes. Stir in the mozzarella and pecorino, with the oregano and salt and pepper to taste. Reduce the heat to low, cover and cook very gently for about 5 minutes.

Meanwhile, cook the fusilli in plenty of boiling salted water. Drain, then immediately turn the fusilli into an ovenproof serving dish. Pour over the sauce, mix well, then place the dish in the oven for 5 minutes. Serve immediately.

SPAGHETTI WITH RAW TOMATO SAUCE

Illustrated on page 33

This sauce is infinitely superior if made with home-grown tomatoes, or imported plum tomatoes, which have so much more flavour than most of the tomatoes found in the shops in this country. The fruity and rich flavour of rich virgin olive oil is also vital for the final result.

───────── SERVES 4 ─────────

12 oz (340 g) spaghetti or spaghettini
1½ lb (675 g) tomatoes
5 tbls extra virgin olive oil
1 clove garlic, peeled and crushed
1-2 dried chillies
10-12 fresh basil leaves, torn into small pieces
salt and freshly ground black pepper

To skin the tomatoes, plunge them into a saucepan of boiling water, leave for 20 seconds, then plunge into cold water. Peel off the skins.

Cut the tomatoes into thin strips, discarding the seeds. Put the strips into a large serving bowl and add all the remaining ingredients, except the spaghetti. Stir lightly, then leave to stand for at least 3 hours.

Check the seasoning. Remove and discard the chilli.

Cook the spaghetti in plenty of boiling salted water. Drain, then turn immediately into the bowl with the tomatoes. Toss well and serve immediately.

FLAMING PASTA IN TOMATO SAUCE

If you want to make your first course a conversation stopper, serve this pasta. The flaming, of course, is optional. If you do not want to do it, put 1½ tablespoons of vodka straight into the sauce and forget about the show.
For a main course, grilled sausages go well with this pasta. Choose pork chipolatas which do not contain too many herbs or spices, which would kill the taste of the pasta. Grilled steaks are good with it too.

——— SERVES 4 ———

12 oz (340 g) gnocchi or conchiglie (green if liked)
plain tomato sauce (page 77)
3 tablespoons double cream
6 tablespoons vodka
1 oz (25 g) butter

Cook the pasta in plenty of boiling salted water. Meanwhile, heat the tomato sauce and when it begins to bubble, mix in the cream and 1 tablespoon of the vodka. Cook for 2 minutes, stirring very frequently. Check the seasoning.

Drain the pasta, then immediately return it to the pan in which it was cooked. Toss it with the butter, then very thoroughly mix in the tomato and cream sauce. Transfer the pasta to a heated serving dish.

Heat the remaining vodka in a soup ladle until it is nearly boiling. Bring the dish quickly to the table. Pour the vodka over the pasta and set fire to it. Toss quickly and serve.

SMALL MACARONI WITH AUBERGINE AND TOMATO SAUCE

Illustrated on pages 34/35

However glossy, firm and fresh the aubergines you buy in this country may be, I recommend peeling them, because the skin is usually tough. You can salt the aubergines for longer than 1 hour if you wish.

——— SERVES 4 ———

12 oz (340 g) small macaroni or pipe rigate
1 aubergine, weighing about 1 lb 5 oz (600 g)
salt and freshly ground black pepper
6 tablespoons olive oil
2 cloves garlic, peeled and chopped
1 lb (450 g) fresh ripe tomatoes, skinned, seeded and chopped or
14 oz (400 g) tinned tomatoes, drained and coarsely chopped.
for the garnish
6-7 fresh basil leaves, roughly torn
½ tablespoon oregano

Peel and cut the aubergine into 1 × ¼-in (2.5 cm × 6-mm) strips. Put the strips into a colander, sprinkle liberally with salt, toss and leave to stand on a plate for at least 1 hour. Rinse under cold running water and dry thoroughly with kitchen paper.

Heat the oil with the garlic in a large, heavy frying pan, add the aubergine and cook for 5 minutes over a moderate heat, stirring frequently.

Add the tomatoes, with salt, if necessary, and pepper to taste, and cook for about 15 minutes, stirring frequently.

Meanwhile, cook the macaroni in plenty of boiling salted water. Drain, then immediately turn into a heated serving bowl. Spoon over the sauce and mix well. Sprinkle with the basil and oregano and serve immediately.

Above: Flaming Pasta (in this case, lumache) in Tomato Sauce.

SPAGHETTI AND ASPARAGUS TIPS IN A TOMATO SAUCE

The asparagus for this dish is not pre-cooked, so use the thin green 'sprue' asparagus. Asparagus should be used at the beginning or height of the season, not at the end when it becomes stringy and hard.

SERVES 4

---

12 oz (340 g) spaghetti or linguine
2 lb (900 g) thin asparagus
5 tablespoons olive oil
14 oz (400 g) tinned tomatoes
salt and freshly ground black pepper
for serving
freshly grated Parmesan cheese

Cut the tips off the asparagus spears, to a length of about 2 in (5 cm) and reserve the remainder for making soup. Wash and dry the tips, reserve half a dozen and cut the remainder into ½-in (1-cm) pieces.

Heat the oil in a saucepan until warm, not too hot, add the asparagus tips and sauté for 2 minutes, stirring very gently. Use a fork to carefully move the pieces around the saucepan; try not to damage the tips.

Purée the tomatoes with their juice in a food mill or pass them through a sieve. Add the tomato purée to the pan, with salt and pepper to taste. Cover and cook until the asparagus tips are tender, stirring frequently, but gently. If the sauce becomes too dry, add 2 or 3 tablespoons of the water in which the pasta is cooking. Reserve the larger tips for garnish.

Meanwhile, cook the pasta in plenty of boiling salted water. Drain, then immediately turn the pasta into a heated serving bowl.

Toss the pasta gently with the sauce, garnish with the longer tips and serve immediately, accompanied by a bowl of grated Parmesan.

PASTA WITH BROAD BEANS

You can use frozen broad beans or fresh broad beans for this nourishing and rustic, yet delicious, pasta dish. Do not worry if some of the beans break during the cooking.

SERVES 4

---

12 oz (340 g) conchiglie or ditali
2 lb (900 g) fresh broad beans, or 1 lb (450 g) frozen broad beans
6 tablespoons olive oil
1 small onion, very finely chopped
2 cloves garlic, peeled and very finely chopped
1 dried chilli
salt and freshly ground black pepper
4 tablespoons freshly grated pecorino romano or Parmesan cheese

---

Shell the broad beans. If using frozen beans, allow to thaw completely, then remove the skins.

Put 4 tablespoons of the oil and the onion into a large heavy frying pan and sauté very gently for 5 minutes. Mix in the garlic and chilli and cook for a further 30 seconds, stirring constantly. If using fresh broad beans, add them to the pan, sprinkle with salt and cook for about 5 minutes, stirring frequently. Add a few tablespoons of hot water during the cooking, not more than a couple at a time, since the beans should cook in very little liquid. When the beans are tender, remove and discard the chilli, cover the pan and keep warm. (If using frozen beans, the cooking time will be slightly shorter.)

Meanwhile, cook the pasta in plenty of boiling salted water. Drain, reserving a cupful of the cooking liquid, then immediately turn the pasta into the frying pan. Add the remaining oil and enough of the reserved cooking water to moisten. Stir-fry for about 1 minute, then sprinkle with the cheese and serve immediately.

Below: Spaghetti and Asparagus tips in a Tomato Sauce, top: Pasta (in this case, conchiglie) with Broad Beans.

Below: Penne with Brussels sprouts, top: Tonnarelli with Raw Pepper Sauce.

PENNE WITH BRUSSELS SPROUTS

This recipe is particularly good with short pasta shapes, such as penne, conchiglie or the less common orecchiette, which means 'little ears'. The durum wheat flour from which it is made gives a very difficult dough to handle, but orecchiette is now a manufactured pasta shape which you can buy in many shops.

———————— SERVES 4 ————————

12 oz (340 g) penne or orecchiette
1 lb (450 g) Brussels sprouts, very small and compact, trimmed
2 tablespoons olive oil
1-2 cloves garlic, peeled and sliced
a small piece of dried chilli, finely chopped
4 oz (120 g) smoked streaky bacon rashers, rinds removed, and cut into matchsticks
salt and freshly ground black pepper
4 tablespoons double cream
4 tablespoons freshly grated Parmesan cheese

Cook the sprouts in 7 pints (4 litres) salted boiling water for 5 minutes. Remove with a slotted spoon and transfer to a colander to drain. Reserve the cooking water.

Heat the oil in a large frying pan and sauté the garlic and chilli for 30 seconds. Add the bacon and cook over a low heat for a further 5 minutes, stirring frequently. Be careful not to let the garlic burn.

Meanwhile, set aside a handful of the best sprouts and cut the remainder into thin strips. Add the shredded sprouts to the pan and sauté gently for a few minutes. Add about 4 tablespoons reserved cooking water, cover and cook over a low heat, until the sprouts are soft.

Return the reserved water to the boil and cook the pasta in it. Drain, reserving a few tablespoons of the water, then immediately turn the pasta into the frying pan. Add the cream, the Parmesan and plenty of black pepper and stir-fry for 1 minute. If the dish seems too dry, add a couple of tablespoons reserved cooking water and mix well. Serve immediately.

TONNARELLI WITH RAW PEPPER SAUCE

I find that some nuova cucina recipes are too remote from traditional Italian taste for my liking. This sauce, however, has an authentic Italian flavour, while the combination of the ingredients and the texture is distinctly nuova cucina.

———————— SERVES 4 ————————

tonnarelli made with 3 eggs and 11 oz (300 g) strong flour (page 6); or 1 lb (450 g) shop-bought fresh spaghetti; or 12 oz (340 g) dried egg tagliatelle
2 large red and/or yellow peppers
2 hard-boiled egg yolks
1 tablespoon capers, rinsed
1 tablespoon green peppercorns
1 small clove garlic, peeled
5 tablespoons olive oil
salt and freshly ground black pepper (optional)

Cut the peppers into quarters, removing all the seeds and membrane. Using a swivel-action peeler, remove and discard as much of the pepper skin as possible. Wash the pepper flesh and dry thoroughly with kitchen paper. Cut into small pieces.

Put the chopped peppers into a food processor or blender with the egg yolks, capers, peppercorns and garlic, and process until smooth. Gradually pour the oil through the funnel while the machine is running. Season to taste with salt and pepper, if used. Transfer the pepper mixture to an ovenproof serving bowl.

Place in a very low oven 225°F (110°C, gas mark ¼).

Cook the tonnarelli in plenty of boiling salted water. Drain, then immediately turn the tonnarelli into the bowl with the pepper sauce. Toss gently but thoroughly and serve immediately.

29

PEPPERS STUFFED WITH DITALINI

For this recipe some cooks prefer to put the peppers in a hot oven for a few minutes to loosen the skin prior to peeling them. However, since I love the taste of grilled peppers, I prefer to grill them to loosen the skin, although it takes longer.

—————— SERVES 4 ——————

4 oz (120 g) ditalini or other small pasta
4 large yellow or red peppers
salt
4 tablespoons olive oil
2 salted anchovies, boned and washed, or 4 tinned anchovy fillets
½ garlic clove, peeled
½ small dried chilli
a small bunch of parsley
1 teaspoons oregano
1 tablespoon capers, rinsed
for the garnish
8 black olives, stoned and cut into strips

Wash and dry the peppers. Place them under a hot grill and cook, turning from time to time, until the skins are charred black all over. Put each pepper into a polythene bag and leave to cool, to make peeling easier.

Remove the peppers from the bags and wipe them with kitchen paper to remove the skins. Cut each pepper in half lengthways, remove the core and place them close together, cut side up, in an oiled roasting tin.

Cook the pasta in plenty of boiling salted water. Drain when very al dente and dry roughly with kitchen paper. Turn into a bowl and toss with 1 tablespoon of the oil.

Heat the oven to 425°F (220°C, gas mark 7).

Chop together the anchovies, garlic, chilli, parsley, oregano and capers. Transfer to a small bowl and mix in the remaining oil.

Stir the mixture into the cooked pasta and check the seasoning. Use to fill the pepper halves and cook in the oven for 15 minutes. Remove and let stand for about 5 minutes, then serve garnished with the olive strips.

TAGLIATELLE WITH LEEK PUREE AND CREAM

Illustrated on page 33

The vermouth and wine used in this recipe counterbalance the sweetness of the leeks.

—————— SERVES 4 ——————

tagliatelle made with 3 eggs and 11 oz (300 g) strong flour (page 6); or 1 lb (450 g) shop-bought fresh tagliatelle; or 12 oz (340 g) dried egg tagliatelle
1 lb (450 g) cleaned leeks
2 oz (50 g) butter
3 tablespoons dry white vermouth
3 tablespoons dry white wine
salt and freshly ground black pepper
5 fl oz (150 ml) single cream
2½ oz (70 g) Parmesan cheese, freshly grated

Cut the leeks into ¼-in (6-mm) rings and wash.

Melt the butter in a large heavy frying pan, add the leeks and sauté for 2 minutes, turning them over and over in the butter.

Add the vermouth, wine and salt to the pan and continue cooking gently until the leeks are very tender. If they get too dry add a couple of tablespoons of hot water during cooking. Transfer the leeks to a food processor or a liquidizer and process to a smooth purée.

Spoon the leek purée into a saucepan. Add plenty of pepper and the cream, and bring the sauce to a light simmer. Cook for 5 minutes, stirring constantly, then transfer the sauce to a large heated serving bowl. Stir in 2 tablespoons of the Parmesan, cover and keep warm.

Cook the tagliatelle in plenty of boiling salted water. Drain, reserving a cupful of the cooking water, and immediately turn the tagliatelle into the bowl with the leek purée. Add a little of the reserved water and about 2 tablespoons of the remaining Parmesan. Toss very thoroughly and serve immediately, accompanied by the remaining Parmesan in a bowl.

Above: Peppers stuffed with Ditalini.

FARFALLE WITH SPINACH AND CHEESE SAUCE

The flavour of this dish is really most pleasing and delicate. Cheese and spinach blend beautifully together and the nutmeg gives the spinach the necessary strength to balance the cheese flavour.

────────── SERVES 4 ──────────

12 oz (340 g) farfalle
3½ oz (100 g) Gruyère cheese
3½ oz (100 g) Gouda cheese
a thin béchamel sauce (page 76) made with 1½ oz (40 g) butter, 2 tbls flour and 18 fl oz (500 ml) milk
grated nutmeg
salt and freshly ground black pepper
10 oz (280 g) cooked fresh spinach, chopped, or frozen spinach, thawed and chopped

Grate the cheeses on the coarse blade of a grater or chop them in a food processor. Stir the cheeses into the béchamel sauce in a saucepan and season with a very generous grating of nutmeg and salt and pepper to taste. Cook over a very gentle heat, stirring, until the cheeses are melted.

Mix the spinach into the cheese sauce and cook gently to heat through. Check the seasoning. Transfer the sauce to a serving bowl, cover and keep warm in a very low oven 225°F (110°C, gas mark ¼).

Cook the farfalle in plenty of boiling salted water. Drain, reserving a cupful of the cooking water.

Immediately turn the pasta into the bowl with the spinach and cheese sauce and toss well. If the dish seems too dry, spoon in a little of the reserved cooking water and mix thoroughly. Serve immediately.

TAGLIATELLE WITH MUSHROOMS AND CREAM

Illustrated on page 37

The addition of dried porcini to cultivated mushrooms provides the fillip for this north Italian sauce.

────────── SERVES 4 ──────────

tagliatelle made with 3 eggs and 11 oz (300 g) strong flour (page 6); or 1 lb (450 g) shop-bought fresh tagliatelle
1 oz (25 g) dried porcini (wild mushrooms)
2 oz (50 g) butter
1 tablespoon olive oil
1 clove garlic, peeled and bruised
8 oz (225 g) cultivated mushrooms, thinly sliced
salt and freshly ground black pepper
7 fl oz (200 ml) single cream
for serving
2 oz (50 g) freshly grated Parmesan cheese

Soak the porcini in a cupful of warm water for 30 minutes then remove carefully. Rinse under cold running water, then pat dry and cut them into small pieces.

Strain the mushroom soaking liquid through a sieve lined with muslin or kitchen paper and reserve.

Heat the butter and oil in a frying pan, then add the garlic and fry until golden. Mix in the chopped porcini with about half the soaking liquid. Cook for 5 minutes.

Remove and discard the garlic, add the cultivated mushrooms and season. Stir over a moderate heat for 5 minutes, until the liquid has partly evaporated.

Stir in the cream and bring to the boil. Simmer gently for 1 minute, stirring constantly. Check the seasoning. Cover and keep warm over a saucepan of hot water.

Meanwhile, cook the tagliatelle in boiling salted water. Drain, reserving a cupful of the cooking water. Turn the pasta into a heated serving dish and spoon over the sauce. If the dish seems too dry add a few tablespoons of the reserved water. Toss well and serve accompanied by the Parmesan in a bowl.

Above: Fusilli with Tomato and Mozzarella Sauce (page 23).

Above: Farfalle with Spinach and Cheese Sauce.

Above: Spaghetti with Raw Tomato Sauce (page 23).

Above: Tagliatelle with Leek Purée and Cream (page 30).

Left: Small Macaroni with Aubergine and Tomato Sauce (page 24),
right: Pasta (in this case, spaghetti) with Mixed Vegetables.

PASTA WITH MIXED VEGETABLES

This recipe is based on the risotto primavera created by Cipriani of Venice and now justly renowned worldwide.

SERVES 4
---

12 oz (340 g) gnocchetti sardi, spaghetti or short-cut macaroni
4 oz (100 g) French beans, topped and tailed
1 carrot, peeled and diced
4 oz (100 g) fresh garden peas (shelled weight), or frozen petits pois, thawed
1 courgette, diced
1 oz (25 g) butter
3 tablespoons olive oil
2 shallots or 1 small onion, very thinly sliced
1 clove garlic, peeled and sliced
1 tablespoon chopped parsley
1 small stalk celery, finely sliced
¼ chicken stock cube, crumbled
salt and freshly ground black pepper
for serving
freshly grated Parmesan cheese

Cut the beans into ½-in (1-cm) lengths. Plunge them into a saucepan of boiling salted water, add the carrot and cook for 7-10 minutes or until al dente. Remove with a slotted spoon and drain on kitchen paper.

Add the peas to the boiling water and cook until just tender. Remove with a slotted spoon and drain on kitchen paper. Add the courgette to the boiling water and cook for 3 minutes. Remove and drain.

Heat the butter and 2 tablespoons of the oil in a large heavy frying pan. Add the onion, garlic, parsley and celery and sauté for 5 minutes, stirring frequently. Add the stock cube, mix in the blanched vegetables and cook for a further 3 minutes. Check the seasoning.

Meanwhile, cook the pasta in plenty of boiling salted water, drain, then immediately turn the pasta into the frying pan. Stir-fry for 1 minute and serve immediately, accompanied by a bowl of grated Parmesan.

CONCHIGLIE WITH FENNEL

Stewing fennel in butter and milk brings out its flavour, which is emphasized by the cream and Parmesan added at the end of this recipe.
I never blanch fennel. I cannot see the point of throwing away any of its delicious flavour and goodness. When you buy fennel, choose round, squat bulbs which are sweeter and more aromatic.

────────── SERVES 4 ──────────

12 oz (340 g) conchiglie or gnocchi
2 large fennel bulbs, total weight about 1 lb (450 g)
2 oz (50 g) butter
½ pint (150 ml) milk
salt and freshly ground white pepper
½ pint (150 ml) single cream
4 tablespoons freshly grated Parmesan cheese
for serving
freshly grated Parmesan cheese

────────────────────────────

Cut off and discard the tops and any wilted or bruised parts of the fennel. Reserve about 2 tablespoons of the green feathery leaves. Wash and chop it coarsely.

Cut the fennel bulbs into quarters, then into wedges about ¼ in (6 mm) thick. Wash thoroughly in cold water and dry with kitchen paper.

Heat half the butter in a large heavy frying pan until it begins to foam. Add the fennel and sauté for 5 minutes. Add the milk and sprinkle with salt. Reduce the heat to very low, cover and cook for about 20 minutes, until tender, stirring from time to time. Add a little hot milk or water if the fennel gets too dry.

When the fennel is very tender, break it up with a fork, to make a thin yet coarse purée. Stir in the cream and season with plenty of pepper. Cook over a very gentle heat for 2 minutes, stirring very often, then blend in the Parmesan. Cover the pan and set aside.

Meanwhile, cook the pasta in plenty of boiling salted water. Drain, then immediately return it to the pan in which it was cooked. Toss immediately with the re-

maining butter. Spoon over the sauce and mix thoroughly. Turn the pasta into a heated serving dish and sprinkle with the reserved fennel leaves. Serve immediately, with the extra Parmesan separately in a bowl.

PASTA WITH COURGETTES

Illustrated on page 38

I like to make this dish with dried green pasta, which is now sold in many supermarkets and specialist shops. The taste is the same as that of ordinary pasta, but the colour makes a change and it is very attractive with the courgette rounds.

────────── SERVES 4 ──────────

12 oz (340 g) green conchiglie or gnocchi
1 clove garlic, peeled and chopped
5 tablespoons olive oil
1 lb courgettes, sliced
2 teaspoon oregano
salt and freshly ground black pepper
6 tablespoons single cream

────────────────────────────

Put the garlic and oil into a large heavy frying pan and sauté for 1 minute. Mix in the courgettes and cook for 5 minutes, then stir in the oregano. Cook for a further 5-10 minutes, until soft. Gently mix in the cream. Season with salt and plenty of pepper.

Meanwhile, cook the pasta in plenty of boiling salted water. Drain, then immediately turn it into a heated serving bowl. Pour over the sauce, toss well and serve immediately.

Below: Conchiglie with Fennel, top: Tagliatelle with Mushrooms and Cream (page 32).

Left: Pasta (in this case, conchiglie) with Courgettes (page 36), right: Paglia e Fieno with Onion Sauce.

PAGLIA E FIENO
WITH ONION SAUCE

This delectable sauce for paglia e fieno (which means 'straw and hay'), or any other egg pasta, such as tagliatelle, is very simple to make, but it takes a long time to cook. You can prepare it in advance, and keep it in the refrigerator for up to 4 days, or freeze it.

───────── SERVES 4 ─────────

8 oz (225 g) shop-bought fresh paglia e fieno
1 oz (25 g) butter
3 tablespoons olive oil
1 lb (450 g) onions, very finely sliced
1 teaspoon sugar
salt and freshly ground black pepper
5 tablespoons dry white wine
1 tablespoon vegetable oil
6 tablespoons single cream
3 oz (85 g) Parmesan cheese, freshly grated

───────────────────────

Heat the butter and oil in a heavy saucepan. Add the onions, sprinkle with the sugar and salt to taste. Cover and cook over a very low heat for about 1 hour, stirring occasionally, and adding a little boiling water, if necessary, until the onion is a thick purée.

Raise the heat and add the wine. Allow to bubble until evaporated, then season with pepper. Add salt to taste. Cook for a further few minutes.

Meanwhile, bring a large saucepan of salted water to the boil, add the vegetable oil and cook the paglia e fieno very briefly. Drain, reserving a cupful of the cooking water, then immediately turn it into a heated serving bowl. Pour over the sauce and toss well, then add the cream and 2 tablespoons of the Parmesan and toss again. If the dish seems too dry, add a couple of tablespoons of the reserved cooking water and mix well, Serve immediately, accompanied by the remaining Parmesan in a bowl.

TAGLIATELLE
WITH PEAS AND CREAM

Illustrated on page 41

The mixture of garden peas and cream makes a very delicate and well-blended sauce, ideal for fresh or dried tagliatelle. It is also a good sauce for tortellini, fresh or dried.

───────── SERVES 4 ─────────

tagliatelle made with 3 eggs and 11 oz (300 g) strong flour (page 6); or 1 lb (450 g) shop-bought fresh tagliatelle; or 12 oz (340 g) dried egg tagliatelle
1 oz (25 g) butter
1 tablespoons olive oil
1 large onion (about 4 oz/120 g), very finely chopped
½ teaspoon sugar
salt and freshly ground black pepper
8 oz (225 g) garden peas, cooked, or frozen petits pois, thawed, or tinned French or Italian petits pois, drained and rinsed
4 tablespoons chicken stock
1 teaspoons plain flour
7 fl oz (200 ml) single cream
1 teaspoon chopped marjoram or ½ teaspoon dried marjoram
for serving
Parmesan cheese, freshly grated

───────────────────────

Heat the butter and oil in a heavy saucepan and sauté the onion with the sugar and a little salt, until soft. Add the peas and stir over a gentle heat for 30 seconds. Add the stock and cook for 5 minutes. Sprinkle with the flour and cook for 1 further minute, stirring.

Remove the pan from the heat and blend in the cream. Return to the heat and bring slowly to the boil. Add the marjoram and season with pepper. Taste and add salt if necessary. Allow to boil for 1 minute, stirring.

Meanwhile, cook the tagliatelle in plenty of boiling salted water. Drain, then immediately turn it into a heated serving dish. Pour over the sauce, mix well and serve accompanied by the Parmesan in a bowl.

LAGANELLE WITH CHICK-PEAS

Laganelle, a kind of pasta made in Basilicata in southern Italy, are like large tagliatelle. Tinned chick-peas can be successfully used instead of dried ones.

———————— SERVES 6 ————————

home-made laganelle made with 3 eggs and 11 oz (300 g) strong
flour (page 6); or 1 lb 2 oz (500 g) shop-bought fresh tagliatelle; or
14 oz (400 g) dried lasagnette (or mafalde)
8 oz (225 g) dried chick-peas or 14 oz (400 g) tinned chick-peas
1 tablespoon bicarbonate of soda (optional)
1 tablespoons plain flour (optional)
6 tablespoons olive oil
2 cloves garlic, peeled and very finely chopped
½ dried chilli, or more according to taste, seeded and chopped
2 tablespoons chopped parsley
2 teaspoons fresh rosemary needles, very finely chopped, or
1 teaspoon dried rosemary
salt

If using dried chick-peas, put them into a bowl and cover with cold water. Mix the bicarbonate of soda and flour with a little warm water and stir this mixture into the bowl with the chick-peas. (This is optional, but I find it helps to soften the skin of the chick-peas which can be quite tough.) Leave to soak for at least 12 hours.

Heat the oven to 325°F (160°C, gas mark 3).

Rinse the chick-peas thoroughly and put them into a flameproof casserole. Cover with water and bring to the boil. Transfer the casserole to the oven and cook, tightly covered, for 1½-2 hours, depending on freshness, until the chick-peas are tender, then drain.

Put the oil, garlic, parsley, chilli and rosemary into a large heavy frying pan. Sauté for about 2 minutes.

If you are using tinned chick-peas, drain and rinse them. Add the chick-peas to the pan, season to taste with salt and heat through thoroughly, stirring.

Cook the laganelle in plenty of boiling salted water. Drain and immediately turn into a heated serving bowl. Pour over the chick-pea mixture, toss well and serve.

40

SPAGHETTI WITH BLACK TRUFFLES

This utterly delicious pasta dish is the grandest treat you can serve. Truffles are certainly not cheap, but once in a year, a decade or even a lifetime, it is worth eating them. You should use fresh truffles during the winter, although truffles preserved in jars, not in tins, are quite good and can be used in the summer months.

———————— SERVES 4 ————————

12 oz (340 g) spaghetti
3 oz (85 g) black truffles
4 fl oz (110 ml) extra virgin olive oil
3 cloves garlic, peeled and bruised
2 dried chillies
2 tablespoons chopped parsley
salt

If you are using fresh truffles, scrub them gently under cold water and then dry them thoroughly with kitchen paper. If you are using preserved truffles, drain them and dry well. Grate the truffles on the coarse blade of a grater or slice them into tiny slivers.

Put the oil, garlic, chillies and parsley into a large heavy frying pan. Heat slowly, stirring very frequently, until the garlic begins to colour. Remove and discard the garlic and chilli.

Turn the heat down to very low and add the truffles to the pan. Cook very gently for 1 minute, stirring constantly.

Meanwhile, cook the pasta in plenty of boiling salted water. Drain, then immediately turn the pasta into the frying pan. Cook over a very low heat, for about 1 minute, turning the spaghetti over and over to coat in the oil. Serve immediately, straight from the pan.

Top: Tagliatelle with Peas and Cream (page 39), centre: Laganelle with Chick Peas, below: Spaghetti with Black Truffles.

CURRIED PAGLIA E FIENO WITH PRAWNS

Parmesan is seldom added to fish sauces but gives this one a more velvety consistency and a piquant flavour which lightens the strong taste of the curry powder.

―――――― SERVES 4 ――――――

1 lb (450 g) shop-bought fresh paglia e fieno
1 lb (450 g) prawns
3 oz (85 g) butter
4 tablespoons dry white wine
1 tablespoon curry powder
2 egg yolks
¼ pint (150 ml) single cream
1 tablespoon vegetable oil
5 tablespoons freshly grated Parmesan cheese
for serving (optional)
freshly grated Parmesan cheese

Shell the prawns. Reserve a few of the best ones for the garnish and cut the remainder crossways.

Melt half the butter in a small, heavy saucepan, add the chopped prawns and sauté for 30 seconds. Splash with the wine and boil briskly to reduce by half.

Reduce the heat and mix in the curry powder. Cook for 1 minute, then transfer the mixture to the top of a double boiler or to a heatproof bowl which will fit over a saucepan of very hot water.

Beat the egg yolks and cream together in a bowl.

Meanwhile, bring a large saucepan of water to the boil. Add salt and the oil and drop in the paglia e fieno which will be cooked in 45 seconds after the water returns to the boil. Lift out the paglia e fieno with a wooden fork or with a spaghetti lifter and put it straight into the curry sauce. The paglia e fieno should be dripping with water when added to the sauce, or it will become too dry when you beat in the egg yolks.

Add the remaining butter, the cream and yolk mixture and the grated cheese to the pasta and toss until the ingredients are thoroughly mixed. Cook for 1 minute over gently simmering, not boiling, water.

Transfer the paglia e fieno to a heated serving dish, decorate with the reserved prawns and serve immediately. Serve with extra Parmesan separately in a bowl, if you wish.

RIGATONI WITH SCALLOPS

I would have this pasta twice a week if it were not so expensive. You need fresh scallops and perfect timing.

―――――― SERVES 4 ――――――

12 oz (340 g) small rigatoni or small penne
8 scallops, total weight 10-12 oz (275-340 g)
4 fl oz (110 ml) olive oil
2 cloves garlic, peeled and very finely chopped
2 tablespoons chopped parsley
1-2 dried chillies, seeded and chopped
2 oz (50 g) fresh white breadcrumbs, lightly toasted in the oven
salt and freshly ground black pepper

Bring 7 pints (4 litres) of water to the boil in a large saucepan. Meanwhile, clean the scallops, removing the muscle. Wash them and separate the white meat from the coral. Dry thoroughly and cut the white meat and the coral into little cubes.

When the water is boiling, add 2 tablespoons cooking salt and drop in the pasta. Stir and cook as usual.

Five minutes after you have put the pasta into the water, make the sauce. Heat the oil with the garlic, parsley and chilli in a large heavy frying pan. Cook for about 1 minute over a moderate heat, stirring constantly. Mix in the white scallop meat and sauté for 30 seconds, then add the breadcrumbs. Stir carefully for 30 seconds, to coat in the oil. Add salt and pepper to taste. Drain the cooked pasta and immediately turn it into the frying pan. Add the scallop coral and stir-fry for 1 minute. Serve immediately.

Above: Curried Paglia e Fieno with Prawns.

Above: Spaghetti with Clams and Tomato Sauce (page 44)

Above: Rigatoni with Scallops.

Above: Penne with Cauliflower (page 44).

SPAGHETTI WITH CLAMS
Illustrated on page 43

Instead of fresh clams, you can use 14 oz (400 g) tinned clams in brine (not vinegar), or 7 oz (200 g) frozen clams. The sauce is equally good made with mussels.

—————— SERVES 4 ——————

12 oz (340 g) spaghetti
2¼ lb (1 kg) small clams in their shells, cleaned
4 tablespoons dry white wine
14 oz (400 g) tinned tomatoes
5 tablespoons olive oil
1 clove garlic, peeled and very finely chopped
2 tablespoons chopped parsley
salt and freshly ground black pepper

Put the clams and wine into a large heavy frying pan and cook, covered, over a high heat until they open, shaking the pan occasionally.

Remove the clams from the pan, reserving the cooking liquid. Remove the meat from the shells and discard the shells. Unless the clams are very small, cut them into halves or quarters. Reserve.

Strain the clam cooking liquid into a small saucepan through a sieve lined with muslin. Reduce over a high heat until about 7 tablespoons are left. Reserve.

Purée the tomatoes in a fine food mill or pass through a sieve. Heat the oil with the garlic and 1 tablespoon of the parsley in a large heavy frying pan, until the garlic is just coloured. Add the tomato purée to the pan with the clam liquid. Stir, season with a little salt and plenty of pepper, and cook, uncovered, over a moderate heat for 15 minutes, stirring occasionally. Meanwhile, cook the spaghetti in boiling salted water.

Just before the spaghetti is ready, add the clams to the sauce. Reduce the heat to very low and mix thoroughly, just to warm through. Check the seasoning.

Drain the spaghetti as soon as it is cooked and turn it into a heated serving bowl. Spoon over the sauce, toss, and serve sprinkled with the remaining parsley.

PENNE WITH CAULIFLOWER
Illustrated on page 43

In southern Italy, pasta is often dressed with a vegetable-based sauce. This recipe is from Sicily.

—————— SERVES 4 ——————

12 oz (340 g) penne or other medium tubular pasta
1 cauliflower, weighing about 1 lb (450 g), divided into florets
5 tablespoons olive oil
1 onion, very finely sliced
4 tinned anchovy fillets, drained and chopped
2 teaspoons tomato purée
2 tablespoons sultanas soaked and drained
about 6 black and 6 green olives, stoned and cut into strips
2 tablespoons pine nuts
salt and freshly ground black pepper
2 oz (50 g) pecorino romano or Parmesan cheese, freshly grated
for garnish
1 tablespoon chopped parsley

Cook the cauliflower in boiling, salted water for about 5 minutes. Remove with a slotted spoon, set aside a few florets and chop the rest. Reserve the cooking water.

Heat the oil in a frying pan and sauté the onion over a gentle heat until light golden and soft, pressing it onion against the pan to release the juices.

Add the anchovies and cook, stirring, for 30 seconds, then mix in the tomato purée and cook for 1 further minute. Add the chopped cauliflower and cook for a further 10 minutes or so, mashing everything together. The sauce should be like a thick, coarse purée.

Add the sultanas, olives and pine nuts. Cook for 1-2 minutes, stirring gently. Sprinkle with a generous grinding of pepper. Adjust seasoning.

Return the reserved cauliflower water to the boil, adding more water, if necessary, to make up to about 6 pints (3.5 litres). When the water is boiling fast, cook the pasta. Drain, then turn the pasta into a heated dish.

Mix in the sauce and the grated cheese. Top with the reserved cauliflower and sprinkle with the parsley.

SPAGHETTI WITH TOMATOES, ANCHOVIES AND OLIVES

Illustrated on page 47

In Italian, this recipe is now called spaghetti alla puttanesca, a new name for a sauce as old as the profession to which it refers (puttana means prostitute). It is a characteristic Neapolitan sauce, gutsy and quick like the Neapolitans themselves.

———— SERVES 4 ————

12 oz (340 g) spaghetti
1½ lb (675 g) tinned tomatoes
5 tablespoons olive oil
½ small dried chilli, seeded and chopped
2 cloves garlic, peeled and finely sliced
3 salted anchovies, boned, washed and chopped, or 6 tinned anchovy fillets, drained and chopped
4 oz (120 g) black olives, stoned and sliced
1 tablespoon capers, rinsed
salt
1 tablespoon chopped parsley

Purée the tomatoes in a food mill or pass through a sieve. Put the tomato purée and half the oil in a saucepan and cook at a brisk simmer for about 10 minutes, stirring occasionally, until thickened.

Combine the remaining oil, the chilli, garlic, and anchovies in a large heavy frying pan. Sauté over a low heat for about 2 minutes, stirring very frequently and pounding the anchovies to a paste.

Add the tomato sauce to the pan and then mix in the olives, capers and parsley and cook gently for a further 3 minutes. Taste and add salt if necessary.

Meanwhile, cook the spaghetti in plenty of boiling salted water. Drain, then immediately turn the spaghetti into the frying pan. Stir-fry for 1 minute, then serve straight from the pan.

LINGUINE WITH TUNA AND TOMATO SAUCE

Illustrated on page 48

You will need best-quality tuna fish for this sauce. Buy Italian or Spanish tuna, packed in olive oil.

———— SERVES 4 ————

12 oz (340 g) linguine or spaghetti
4 tablespoons olive oil
1 shallot or ½ small onion, very finely chopped
2 cloves garlic, peeled and very finely chopped
1 small stalk celery with leaves, very finely chopped
salt and freshly ground black pepper
½ teaspoon sugar
14 oz (400 g) tinned tomatoes
3 tablespoons dry white wine
7 oz (200 g) tuna fish, drained and flaked
1 teaspoon anchovy purée
1 tablespoon capers, rinsed
12 black olives, stoned and cut into strips
1 tablespoon chopped parsley

Put the oil, shallot, garlic and celery into a heavy saucepan and sauté gently for about 1 minute. Sprinkle with a little salt and the sugar and sauté for a further 3 minutes.

Add the tomatoes with their juice to the pan, bring to the boil and then pour in the wine. Cook at a brisk simmer for 10 minutes, stirring occasionally.

Add the tuna fish to the pan with the anchovy purée. Cook for 5 minutes, then reduce the heat to low and mix in the capers, olives and parsley. Add a generous grinding of pepper, taste and add a little salt if necessary.

Meanwhile, cook the pasta in plenty of boiling salted water. Drain, then immediately turn the pasta into a heated serving bowl. Spoon over the sauce, toss well and serve immediately.

TAGLIATELLE WITH SMOKED SALMON

The idea of combining pasta with foreign ingredients originated with the nuova cucina, *Italian nouvelle cuisine. The sauce in this recipe makes a very successful marriage between* italianissime *tagliatelle and Scotch smoked salmon.*
You can buy salmon trimmings for the sauce, which are cheaper than sliced smoked salmon, but make sure they do not have that all too frequent taste of cod liver oil. If you can, buy the trimmings from a fishmonger who smokes his own salmon.

———————— SERVES 4 ————————

Tagliatelle made with 3 eggs and 11 oz (300 g) strong flour (page 6); or 1 lb (450 g) shop-bought fresh tagliatelle; or 12 oz (340 g) dried egg tagliatelle
2 oz (50 g) butter
1 clove garlic, peeled and bruised
4 fresh sage leaves or 3 dried sage leaves
7 oz (200 g) smoked salmon, cut into 2-in (5-cm) strips
1 oz (25 g) shelled pistachio nuts, blanched, skinned and chopped
½ tablespoon lemon juice
3 tablespoons whisky
7 fl oz (200 ml) single cream
generous pinch of cayenne pepper
salt

Put the butter, garlic and sage into a large heavy frying pan. Heat until the garlic begins to colour, then remove and discard the garlic and sage.

Mix the smoked salmon into the hot butter and toss well. Reserve about half the pistachio nuts and add the remainder to the pan. Sauté for 30 seconds. Add the lemon juice and cook for a further few seconds. Add the whisky and cook for 1 minute. Then add the cream and heat through, stirring constantly, until just below boiling point. Add the cayenne pepper and salt, if necessary. Turn off the heat and cover the pan.

Cook the tagliatelle in plenty of boiling salted water. Drain, reserving a cupful of the cooking water, then immediately turn the pasta into the frying pan with the salmon and whisky sauce. Stir-fry over a gentle heat for 1 minute, adding a couple of tablespoons of the reserved cooking water if the dish seems too dry. Serve immediately on a heated dish.

TAGLIATELLE WITH CAVIAR

I like to serve this dish with Tagliatelle with Smoked Salmon (above). They look pretty together and their flavours combine very well. For this sauce, you do not need the best caviar: a good-quality lumpfish roe will do instead.

———————— SERVES 4 ————————

tagliatelle made with 3 eggs and 11 oz (300 g) strong flour (page 6); or 1 lb (450 g) shop-bought fresh tagliatelle; or 12 oz (340 g) dried egg tagliatelle
2 oz (50 g) butter
5 tablespoons caviar or good-quality black lumpfish roe
2 tablespoons lemon juice
2 tablespoons vodka
4 fl oz (110 ml) soured cream
freshly ground black pepper

Melt the butter in a small saucepan and stir in the caviar and lemon juice. Cook over a moderate heat for 1 minute, stirring constantly. Reduce the heat and add the vodka, soured cream and plenty of pepper. Simmer very gently for 5 minutes, without allowing to boil.

Meanwhile, cook the tagliatelle in plenty of boiling salted water. Drain, reserving a cupful of the cooking water. Immediately transfer the pasta to a heated serving dish and pour over the sauce. Toss thoroughly and, if the dish seems too dry, add a couple of tablespoons of the reserved cooking water and mix well. Serve so that bits of the roe show attractively.

Clockwise, from top left: Tagliatelle with Smoked Salmon; Tagliatelle with Caviar; Spaghetti with Tomatoes, Anchovies and Olives (page 45).

Left: Linguine with Tuna and Tomato Sauce (page 45), right: Vermicelli Nests with Monkfish in Spinach and Sorrel Sauce.

VERMICELLI NESTS WITH MONKFISH IN SPINACH AND SORREL SAUCE

I based this recipe on one which appeared in the excellent Italian magazine La Cucina Italiana. *Vermicelli are usually used in soup, but they are ideal for this dish, both in appearance and texture. Remember that they take only 2 minutes to cook. A handful of sorrel, mixed with the spinach, makes the sauce even more delicious. Unfortunately, sorrel is difficult to find, but it is very easy to grow in the garden. However, if you cannot get it, do not despair; the sauce is excellent even without it. It can be prepared in advance and reheated.*

―――――――― SERVES 4 ――――――――

11 oz (300 g) vermicelli
1½-2 oz (40-50 g) sorrel leaves
3 oz (85 g) butter
5 oz (150 g) cooked spinach
salt and freshly ground black pepper
1 tablespoon lemon juice
¼ pint (150 ml) single cream
2 shallots or 1 small onion, very finely chopped
14 oz (400 g) monkfish, skinned and cut into ½-in (1-cm) cubes
4 fl oz (110 ml) dry white wine
2 teaspoons fresh thyme or 1 teaspoon dried thyme
1 tablespoon vegetable oil

To make the sauce, wash the sorrel and remove the central ribs. Melt half the butter in a small heavy saucepan. Add the sorrel and spinach and cook gently until the butter has been absorbed. Add salt and pepper, and the lemon juice, and cook for 30 seconds, stirring constantly. Stir in the cream and bring to just below boiling point. Transfer the mixture to a blender or food processor and blend until reduced to a creamy purée.

Return the sauce to the pan, cover and keep warm in a bain marie or in a low oven 250°F (120°C, gas mark ½). Put the remaining butter and the shallots in a frying pan and sauté until the shallot is soft. Add the monkfish and sauté for 30 seconds, turning it over and over in the butter.

Heat the wine and pour it over the fish. Cook for 2 minutes, add the thyme, then turn off the heat. Cover the pan and keep warm in a low oven.

Bring a large saucepan of salted water to the boil and add the vegetable oil. Drop the vermicelli nests into the water one at a time, stirring briskly with a fork to prevent them from sticking together. Drain the vermicelli nests, reserving a cupful of the cooking water, then immediately return them to the pan in which they were cooked.

Using a metal fork, roll up nests of vermicelli, allowing 3 for each person, and set them on individual heated plates. Pour a little of the reserved cooking water into each nest, just to moisten. Place the monkfish in the middle of the nests and spoon over the fish cooking juices.

Reheat the spinach and cream sauce, if necessary, and spoon a little on to each plate. Serve immediately.

Left: Spaghetti and Steak in Pizza Sauce (page 52), top: Macaroni with Curried Chicken (page 52), right: Tagliatelle with Veal.

TAGLIATELLE WITH VEAL

This is a recipe which originates from Alto Adige in north-eastern Italy, where pasta is often served with meat as a main course. The cooking of Alto Adige has a strong Austrian influence as, until 1918, it was part of the Austro-Hungarian Empire.

--- SERVES 6 ---

tagliatelle made with 3 eggs and 11 oz (300 g) strong flour (page 6); or 1 lb 2 oz (500 g) shop-bought fresh tagliatelle; or 14 oz (400 g) dried egg tagliatelle
2 tablespoons vegetable oil
3 oz (85 g) butter
1 large onion, chopped
2¼ lb (1 kg) leg of veal, boned and cut into 1 in (2.5-cm) cubes
10 fresh sage leaves or 1 teaspoon dry sage
2 tablespoons tomato purée
1 tablespoon plain flour
1 tablespoon Hungarian paprika
¼ pint (150 ml) dry white wine
¼ pint (150 ml) beef stock
salt and freshly ground black pepper

Heat the oil and 1 oz (25 g) of the butter in a flameproof casserole and sauté the onion until soft.

Add the veal, sage, tomato purée, flour and paprika, and cook over a moderate heat, stirring constantly, for 1 minute. Add the wine and boil briskly for 2 minutes, turning the veal over and over. Pour in the stock, add salt and pepper and bring to the boil. Reduce the heat to very low, cover the casserole and simmer for about 1 hour. If the sauce gets too dry, add 3-4 tablespoons hot water.

When the veal is nearly ready, cook the tagliatelle in plenty of boiling, salted water. Drain, then immediately turn into a heated serving dish, add the remaining butter and toss well. Mix in half the sauce, toss well again and surround with the veal stew and the remaining sauce. Serve immediately.

SPAGHETTI AND STEAK IN PIZZA SAUCE
Illustrated on pages 50/51

The sauce for this meat and pasta dish is reminiscent of a Neapolitan pizza topping.

———— SERVES 4 ————

11 oz (300 g) spaghetti
1 lb (450 g) rump or frying steak
4 tbls olive oil
1 lb 6 oz (620 g) tinned chopped tomatoes
2 oz (50 g) black olives, stoned and cut into strips
2 cloves garlic, very finely chopped
1 tablespoon chopped parsley
2 tablespoons capers
salt and fresh ground black pepper

Cut the meat into thin strips about 2 in (5 cm) long by ½ in (1 cm) wide. Heat 2 tablespoons of the oil in a heavy frying pan. Add the meat and cook over a high heat for 1 minute. Remove the meat with a slotted spoon and transfer to a plate.

Add all the remaining ingredients except the remaining oil to the pan and cook over a moderate heat for about 10 minutes, stirring frequently, until the sauce is quite thick.

Meanwhile, cook the spaghetti in plenty of boiling salted water. Just before it is ready, return the meat with all its juice to the frying pan and heat through gently. Check the seasoning.

Drain the spaghetti, then immediately return it to the saucepan in which it was cooked. Toss with the remaining oil and with a few tablespoons of the meat and tomato sauce. Turn on to a heated serving dish and pour the remaining meat and sauce around it. Serve immediately.

MACARONI WITH CURRIED CHICKEN
Illustrated on pages 50/51

This is an ideal way of using leftover roast chicken. The result is simply delicious and quite unusual. You can also use chicken or turkey fillets of breast, lightly sautéed in butter.

———— SERVES 4 ————

11 oz (300 g) macaroni or penne
2 oz (50 g) butter
2-3 tablespoons curry powder
4 fl oz (110 ml) dry white wine
2 tablespoons milk
2 cloves garlic, peeled and bruised
1 bay leaf
1 tablespoon sunflower oil
salt
1 tablespoon brandy
4 fl oz (110 ml) double cream
1½ oz (40 g) flaked almonds
8 oz (225 g) cooked chicken, white meat only, boned, skinned and cut into strips

Combine the butter, curry powder to taste, wine, milk, garlic, bay leaf, oil and salt to taste in a heavy saucepan. Cook over low heat for 15 minutes, stirring occasionally.

Add the brandy, cream, flaked almonds and all but a few strips of chicken to the pan. Bring to the boil, then reduce the heat and simmer for 3 minutes, stirring constantly. Remove and discard the garlic and bay leaf. Check the seasoning, cover and keep warm.

Meanwhile, cook the pasta in plenty of boiling salted water. Drain, then immediately turn the pasta into a heated serving dish. Spoon over the sauce, toss well and arrange the remaining strips of chicken on top. Serve immediately.

FETTUCCINE WITH HAM RAGU
Illustrated on page 54

This is a variation of the Roman dish garofolato, *based on a piece of beef stuck with cloves and braised. Here beef stock and the traditional vegetables combine in a simple alternative.*

———— SERVES 4 ————

fettuccine made with 3 eggs and 11 oz (300 g) strong flour (page 6); or 1 lb (450 g) shop-bought fresh fettuccine or tagliatelle; or 12 oz (340 g) dried egg tagliatelle
8 oz (225 g) unsmoked fatty ham, cut into matchstick strips
2 tablespoons olive oil
1 small onion, chopped
1 small carrot, chopped
1 stalk celery, chopped
2 cloves garlic, peeled and chopped
1 tablespoon chopped parsley
3-4 cloves
4 fl oz (110 ml) dry white wine
1½ tablespoons tomato purée
4-5 tablespoons strong beef stock
salt and freshly ground black pepper
for serving
freshly grated Parmesan cheese

Put the ham and oil into a large, heavy saucepan and heat until the fat runs. Add all the vegetables, the garlic and parsley, and the cloves wrapped in a small piece of muslin. Cook, stirring very frequently, for 10 minutes.

Pour over the wine, boil briskly for 1 minute, then add the tomato purée stirred into the stock. Season to taste with salt and pepper and cook over a low heat for about 30 minutes, stirring occasionally. The sauce should be thick, but if it seems dry, add a little hot water.

Meanwhile, cook the pasta in plenty of boiling, salted water. Drain, then immediately turn the pasta into a heated serving bowl. Discard the cloves, then pour the sauce over the pasta. Toss well and serve immediately, accompanied by the grated Parmesan in a bowl.

DITALINI WITH BEANS AND SALAMI
Illustrated on page 54

The salami for this recipe must be a soft, coarse-grained Italian salami, such as Romano or Varzi. It should be sliced not too thinly and then cut into matchstick strips. The dish is deliciously robust and earthy.

———— SERVES 4 ————

11 oz (300 g) ditalini or other short tubular pasta
6 tablespoons olive oil
2 cloves garlic, peeled and very finely chopped
a small piece of dried chilli, finely chopped
6 fresh sage leaves, finely chopped, or ½ teaspoon dried sage
8 oz (225 g) tinned tomatoes
salt
14 oz (400 g) tinned cannellini beans
4 oz (120 g) salami, sliced and cut into matchstick strips

Put the oil, garlic, chilli and sage into a large heavy frying pan and heat gently for about 1 minute, stirring very frequently.

Add the tomatoes with their juice and salt to taste. Break up the tomatoes with a spoon and cook over a moderate heat for 10 minutes, until thickened.

Rinse the cannellini beans under cold running water, drain well and add to the pan. Reduce the heat to low and cook for about 5 minutes, stirring occasionally.

Meanwhile, cook the ditalini in plenty of boiling salted water.

Mix the salami into the bean and tomato sauce. Drain the ditalini as soon as they are cooked and add to the pan. Stir-fry for 1 minute, then check the seasoning. Serve immediately.

Above: Bucatini with Pancetta and Eggs.

Above: Fettuccine with Ham Ragù (page 53).

Above: Ditalini with Beans and Salami (page 53).

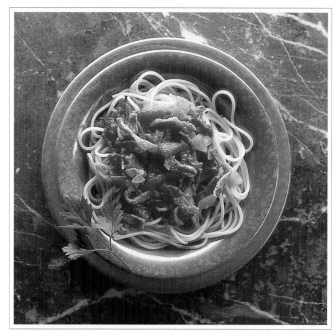

Above: Spaghetti with Bacon, Tomatoes and Chilli.

SPAGHETTI WITH BACON, TOMATOES AND CHILLI

This hot sauce from central Italy is called Amatriciana and often appears on menus in Italian restaurants. Traditionally it is made with pork jowl. You could use salt pork, but unsmoked back bacon is even better.

--- SERVES 4 ---

12 oz (340 g) spaghetti
7 oz (200 g) unsmoked lean bacon rashers, rinded and cut into short matchsticks
3 tablespoons olive oil
2-3 dried chillies, seeded and crumbled
4 tablespoons dry white wine
1 onion, very finely chopped
salt
14 oz (400 g) tinned tomatoes, drained
3 oz (85 g) pecorino romano or Parmesan cheese, freshly grated

Put 2 tablespoons of the oil, the chillies and the bacon into a heavy frying pan. Fry over a moderate heat until the bacon is browned and crispy at the edges, and the fat runs. Splash with the wine and boil briskly to reduce by half.

Reduce the heat to low and add the onion with salt to taste. Cover and cook until the onion is soft, stirring occasionally.

Cut the tomatoes into short strips and add to the pan. Raise the heat slightly and cook for 10 minutes. (Add a little hot water if the sauce gets too dry.) Check the seasoning.

Meanwhile, cook the spaghetti in plenty of boiling salted water. Drain, reserving a cupful of the cooking water, and immediately turn the spaghetti into a heated serving dish. Toss with the remaining oil. Pour over the bacon and tomato sauce, add half the cheese, and toss thoroughly. If the dish seems too dry, add a little of the reserved cooking water and mix well. Serve immediately, accompanied by the remaining cheese in a bowl.

BUCATINI WITH PANCETTA AND EGGS

There are quite a number of variations on this famous Roman sauce, known as carbonara. Some cooks use smoked pancetta, others add more herbs or a dash of white wine. This recipe is the classic version. Use all Parmesan if you cannot find good pecorino romano.

--- SERVES 4 ---

12 oz (340 g) bucatini or spaghetti
1 tablespoon olive oil
3 cloves garlic, peeled and bruised
5 oz (150 g) pancetta or unsmoked streaky bacon, in one slice, cut into thin short strips
3 eggs
2 oz (50 g) freshly grated Parmesan cheese
1 oz (25 g) freshly grated pecorino romano cheese
1 tablespoon chopped parsley
3 tablespoons single cream
½ oz (15 g) butter
salt and freshly ground black pepper

Put the oil and garlic into a small frying pan and sauté until the garlic is coloured, but not brown. Remove and discard the garlic. Add the pancetta to the pan and sauté for about 10 minutes.

Meanwhile, cook the pasta in plenty of boiling salted water.

While the pasta is cooking, lightly beat the eggs in a large bowl and add the cheeses, parsley, cream, butter and a generous grinding of black pepper. Mix well.

Put the bowl at the bottom of a low oven 250°F (120°C, gas mark ½), leaving the door ajar.

When the pasta is cooked, drain and immediately turn it into the bowl with the egg and cheese. Add the hot pancetta, toss well and serve immediately.

PENNE WITH BACON, PEPPERS AND CREAM

I had this sauce in a restaurant in Pavia, a university town and gastronomic centre south of Milan. I was intrigued by the unusual combination of ingredients. It still works marvellously in my version.

--------- SERVES 4 ---------

12 oz (340 g) penne
1 small onion or 1 shallot, very finely chopped
½ oz (15 g) butter
2 tablespoons olive oil
2 large yellow or red peppers
salt and freshly ground black pepper
4 oz (120 g) smoked streaky bacon rinds removed and cut into matchsticks
8 fl oz (225 ml) single cream
for serving
freshly grated Parmesan cheese

Cook the onion in the butter and oil over a low heat, stirring very frequently, for about 7 minutes, until soft.

Meanwhile, wash and dry the peppers. Cut them into quarters, remove the seeds and membrane and cut into matchsticks. Add the peppers to the pan and cook over a moderate heat, stirring frequently, for 10 minutes.

Add the bacon to the pan and fry for 5 minutes, turning the contents of the pan over and over. Season carefully with salt (the bacon will be salty), and a very generous grinding of pepper. Reduce the heat to low, cover the pan and cook for a further 5 minutes, until the peppers are tender.

Meanwhile, cook the penne in plenty of boiling, salted water. A few minutes before the penne are ready, stir the cream into the pepper and bacon sauce and heat through for 1 minute. Check the seasoning.

Drain the penne and immediately turn them into a heated serving bowl. Spoon over the sauce, toss very well and serve, accompanied by the Parmesan.

GREEN TAGLIATELLE WITH PROSCIUTTO AND CREAM

This is a classic sauce, prosciutto and cream being two ingredients which go together beautifully. It is given an extra subtle dimension by the onion and wine.

--------- SERVES 4 ---------

green tagliatelle made with 2 eggs and 7 oz (200 g) strong flour and 5 oz (140 g) cooked spinach (page 6); or 1 lb (450 g) shop-bought fresh green tagliatelle; or 12 oz (340 g) dried egg tagliatelle
2 oz (50 g) butter
1 shallot or ½ small onion, very finely chopped
7 oz (200 g) prosciutto, cut into thick slices
4 tablespoons dry white wine
7 fl oz (200 ml) single cream
freshly ground black pepper
3 oz (85 g) freshly grated Parmesan cheese

Heat the butter with the shallot in a heavy saucepan over a low heat. Cook for about 5 minutes, stirring frequently.

Meanwhile, cut the prosciutto into matchstick lengths, then add to the shallot. Cook for 5 minutes over a low heat.

Add the wine, raise the heat and bubble for 30 seconds. Reduce the heat to low, stir in the cream and add a generous grinding of pepper. Cook very gently for 2 minutes, stirring frequently. Do not allow to boil. Check the seasoning. Pour the sauce into a heated serving bowl and stir in 4 tablespoons of the Parmesan.

Keep warm in a low oven 225°F (110°C, gas mark low).

Cook the tagliatelle in plenty of boiling, salted water. Drain, reserving a cupful of the cooking water, then immediately turn the tagliatelle into the bowl with the sauce and toss thoroughly. If the dish seems too dry, add a couple of tablespoons of the reserved cooking water and mix well. Serve immediately, accompanied by the remaining Parmesan in a bowl.

Left: Penne with Bacon, Peppers and Cream, top: Green Tagliatelle with Prosciutto and Cream.

Left: Bigoli with Chicken Liver Sauce, right: Fettuccine with Kidneys.

FETTUCCINE WITH KIDNEYS

Calves' kidneys are rightly considered a delicacy in Italy. They are very sweet and do not need any blanching or soaking. If you use lambs' kidneys, which are easier to find in this country, soak them in water and vinegar for 30 minutes or so to get rid of the sometimes rather unpleasant taste.

―――――――――― SERVES 4 ――――――――――

fettuccine made with 2 eggs and 7 oz (200 g) strong flour (page 6); or 11 oz (300 g) shop-bought fresh fettuccine or tagliatelle; or 10 oz (280 g) dried egg tagliatelle
12 oz (340 g) kidneys
3 oz (75 g) butter
2 cloves garlic, peeled and bruised
2 tablespoons plain flour
4 fl oz (110 ml) dry white wine
salt and freshly ground black pepper
6 tablespoons single cream

Remove the fat from the kidneys with a small sharp knife or kitchen scissors. Cut them in half lengthways and then crossways into ½-in (1-cm) slices. Pat dry with kitchen paper.

Heat the butter with the garlic in a frying pan until the garlic is coloured, then remove and discard.

Meanwhile, dust the kidneys all over with the flour. Add them to the pan and cook over a moderate heat for about 1 minute, stirring constantly.

Pour over the wine and boil until reduced by half. Check the seasoning, then add the cream. Cook, stirring constantly, until hot.

While the sauce is cooking, cook the pasta in plenty of boiling, salted water. Drain, then immediately turn the pasta into a heated serving bowl. Spoon over the sauce, toss well and serve immediately.

BIGOLI WITH CHICKEN LIVER SAUCE

Bigoli are a kind of thick spaghetti of Venetian origin. The dough, made with egg and either water or milk, is pressed through a special implement, called a bigolaro. Bigoli are now commercially produced, often made with wholewheat flour. The sauce is Venetian, too.

―――――――――― SERVES 4 ――――――――――

12 oz (340 g) wholewheat spaghetti
9 oz (250 g) fresh chicken livers
2 tablespoons olive oil
1½ oz (40 g) butter
4-5 fresh or dried sage leaves
1 clove garlic, peeled and bruised
2 tablespoons dry white wine
salt and freshly ground black pepper
3 oz (85 g) freshly grated Parmesan cheese

Bring a large saucepan of water to the boil. Add about 1½ tablespoons of cooking salt when it begins to boil.

Meanwhile, trim the chicken livers, removing and discarding any gristle or green particles of gall. Wash and dry the livers well, then cut into small pieces.

Cook the spaghetti in the boiling salted water.

Meanwhile, heat the oil, half the butter, the sage and the garlic in a small frying pan. As soon as the garlic begins to colour, remove and discard it together with the sage.

Add the chicken livers to the pan and sauté briskly for 1 minute. Pour over the wine and let it boil away quickly. Season to taste with salt and pepper. Remove from the heat and keep warm.

When the spaghetti is ready, drain and immediately turn into a heated serving bowl. Toss with the remaining butter and then pour over the sauce. Add half the Parmesan and toss thoroughly. Serve immediately, accompanied by the remaining cheese in a bowl.

OLD-FASHIONED MEAT RAVIOLI

This is the recipe for traditional Milanese ravioli. If you have a hand-cranked machine and a ravioli tray, you can make them quite easily, although they take time.

—————— **MAKES ABOUT 100 RAVIOLI, TO SERVE 3-4** ——————

3 oz (85 g) butter
a sprig of fresh sage or ½ teaspoon dried sage
3½ oz (100 g) freshly grated Parmesan cheese
for the ravioli
homemade pasta made with 2 large eggs and 7 oz (200 g) strong flour (page 6)
for the meat filling
1 oz (25 g) butter
1 small onion, very finely chopped
½ small carrot, very finely chopped
1 small stalk celery, very finely chopped
1 clove garlic, peeled and very finely chopped
½ teaspoon chopped sage
½ teaspoon chopped rosemary
1 lb (450 g) chuck steak, or other braising steak, in a single piece, trimmed of all visible fat
4 fl oz (110 ml) red wine
1 tablespoon tomato purée
¼ pint (150 ml) beef stock
2 cloves
salt and freshly ground black pepper
1½ oz (40 g) white bread, crusts removed
3 tablespoons freshly grated Parmesan cheese
1 egg, beaten

Heat the oven to 300°F (150°C, gas mark 2).

To make the filling, put the butter, onion, carrot, celery, garlic and chopped herbs into a flameproof casserole just large enough to contain the meat snugly. Fry gently for 10 minutes, stirring frequently. Add the meat and cook over a low heat for 5 minutes, turning it over.

Raise the heat to moderate and splash the meat with the wine. Boil until reduced by half, then blend in the tomato purée and pour over the stock. Add the cloves and salt to taste and bring slowly to the boil.

Cover the casserole and cook in the oven for 3 hours, basting occasionally and turning the meat over.

Remove from the oven, allow the meat to cool, then weigh out 4 oz (120 g) of it and chop very finely. Put the chopped meat into a bowl. Reserve the remainder for another dish, such as rissoles or a pasta sauce.

Put the bread into a small bowl and add 5 tablespoons of the strained meat juices. Leave the bread to soak for a few minutes, then mash it with a fork. Add the bread to the chopped meat together with the 3 tablespoons of Parmesan, the egg and pepper to taste. Mix well with your hands. Adjust seasoning.

Make the pasta following the instructions on page 6. Stop rolling the sheets out at the last but one notch. When you have rolled out the first sheet, place it over the ravioli tray, previously dusted with flour, stretching the sheet so that it will cover the whole of the surface. Keep the remaining dough covered. Place little mounds of the filling in each cavity.

Using a thin brush, moisten the edges of each ravioli with cold water. Roll out another sheet of dough and place on top of the filling. Press down gently all over and then press down firmly between each ravioli. (I do this with my fingers).) Gently lift the ravioli and place on a large wooden board, lightly dusted with flour. Continue making the ravioli and transferring them to the board. Now cut around each ravioli with the pastry wheel along the imprint left by the tray.

Cover a corner of the work surface with a clean kitchen cloth, dust lightly with flour and place the cut up ravioli over it, being careful that they do not touch each other. Turn the ravioli over once or twice to dry evenly.

Bring a large saucepan of water to the boil, add 2 tablespoons of salt and then lower in the ravioli. Stir with a wooden spoon, cover and return to the boil. Cook for 6-8 minutes. Meanwhile, melt the butter with the sage in a small saucepan and cook until deep golden.

Using a slotted spoon, transfer the cooked ravioli to a colander to drain. Ladle a batch of ravioli into a heated ovenproof dish or serving bowl, pour over a little of the melted butter and sprinkle with a little Parmesan. Add more ravioli and dress with butter and cheese in layers until all the ingredients are used up. Serve immediately, accompanied by the remaining Parmesan in a bowl.

Above: Old-fashioned Meat Ravioli.

RADICCHIO AND SPAGHETTI SALAD

This attractive and original dish will remind you of the best Mediterranean cooking. You will need sweet, mild olives; ask to taste one before buying, because strong olives are not suitable for this dish. If fresh marjoram is unavailable, use parsley instead. If necessary, you can substitute round lettuce leaves for radicchio.

—————— SERVES 6 ——————

12 oz (340 g) spaghetti
1 large head radicchio
4 oz (120 g) sweet black olives, stoned
6 tablespoons extra virgin olive oil
2 tablespoons chopped marjoram
1 clove garlic, peeled
12 green peppercorns
2 tablespoons capers, rinsed
2 hard-boiled eggs (optional)

Cut the core of the radicchio head crossways and re-move the best of the large outside leaves, unfurling them carefully so that they remain whole. Wash and dry them thoroughly. Set aside.

Cook the spaghetti in plenty of boiling salted water, remembering that pasta for salads needs to be more al dente than hot pasta. Drain, refresh under cold running water, then drain again thoroughly. Pat dry with kitchen paper and transfer to a bowl. Add 2 tablespoons of the oil and toss well.

Chop together the olives, marjoram, garlic, capers and peppercorns until coarse and grainy. (Do not reduce to a pulp.) Put the mixture into a small bowl and beat in the remaining oil. Spoon the mixture over the pasta and toss very thoroughly. Check the seasoning. Allow to rest for an hour or so for the flavours to develop.

Lay the radicchio leaves on individual plates and fill them with the spaghetti mixture. If you like, you can decorate with the hard-boiled eggs passed through a wire sieve or a fine food mill.

CONCHIGLIETTE, PRAWN AND FENNEL SALAD

This is a lovely pasta salad and it is even more delicious when made with fresh prawns, whose taste is stronger than that of frozen ones.

—————— SERVES 4 ——————

9 oz (250 g) conchigliette or ditali
1 tablespoon sunflower oil
1 hard-boiled egg
juice of ½ large lemon
salt and freshly ground black pepper
5 tablespoons extra virgin olive oil
1 small or ½ large fennel bulb
8 oz (225 g) peeled prawns

Cook the pasta in plenty of boiling salted water, re-membering that pasta for salads needs to be more al dente than hot pasta. Drain, refresh under cold running water, then drain again thoroughly. Pat dry with kitchen paper. Turn the pasta into a serving bowl and toss immediately with the sunflower oil. Set aside until cold.

To make the sauce, separate the egg yolk from the white and press through a wire strainer into a bowl. Add the lemon juice, salt and pepper. Beat well, then add the olive oil drop by drop, beating constantly with a small wire whisk or a fork, until all the oil is absorbed. Check the seasoning.

Remove the stalks and any bruised parts from the outside leaves of the fennel. Set aside the green feath-ery leaves, wash it and chop coarsely. Cut the fennel lengthways into quarters, then crossways into paper-thin slices. Wash quickly and pat dry. Add to the pasta in the bowl. Mix in the prawns and the reserved fennel leaves. Spoon over the sauce and toss very well. Cover with clingfilm and set aside for about 30 minutes.

Serve at room temperature. Pasta salad should never be served chilled.

Clockwise, from top left: Radicchio and Spaghetti Salad; Conchigliette, Prawn and Fennel Salad; Orecchiette, Cheese, Walnut and Celery Salad (page 64); Ruote, Chicken, Ham and Pea Salad (page 64).

ORECCHIETTE, CHEESE, WALNUT AND CELERY SALAD

Illustrated on page 63

The walnut oil in this recipe gives the dressing a subtle taste, but you can substitute olive oil if you wish.

─────── SERVES 4 ───────

9 oz (250 g) orecchiette or other medium tubular pasta
3 tablespoons sunflower oil
2 tablespoons shelled walnut halves
4 oz (120 g) Fontina or Gruyère cheese, cut into small pieces
4 oz (120 g) Bel Paese or mild Cheddar cheese, cut into small pieces
4 oz (120 g) Gorgonzola or Stilton cheese, cut into small pieces
3 tablespoons walnut oil
2 tablespoons celery leaves
4 stalks celery, trimmed and finely diced
2 tablespoons chopped parsley
freshly ground black pepper

Cook the pasta in plenty of boiling salted water, remembering that pasta for salads needs to be more al dente than hot pasta. Drain, refresh under cold running water, then drain again thoroughly. Pat dry with kitchen paper and transfer to a deep serving bowl. Immediately add 2 tablespoons of the sunflower oil, toss well and leave to cool completely.

Blanch the walnuts in boiling water for just 10 seconds, then drain and remove as much of the skins as you can. (If you are short of time, you can omit this step, but peeled walnuts are sweeter.) Chop the walnuts coarsely and set aside.

When the pasta is cold, mix in the cheeses and the oils. Set aside 1 or 2 sprigs of celery leaves and chop the remainder. Add to the bowl together with the walnuts, celery and parsley. Toss well, then add a generous grinding of black pepper. Check the seasoning.

Cover and stand the dish at room temperature (do not chill) for at least 6 hours, to allow the flavours to combine. Garnish with the reserved celery leaves.

RUOTE, CHICKEN, HAM AND PEA SALAD

Illustrated on page 63

You can use three-coloured shop-bought fresh ruote or fusilli for this lovely salad; the taste is just the same as that of plain pasta, but the colour is prettier.

─────── SERVES 4 ───────

9 oz (250 g) shop-bought fresh ruote or fusilli; or 7 oz (200 g) dried ruote or fusilli
1 tablespoon sunflower oil
4 oz (120 g) cooked boneless chicken, skinned and cut into small cubes
2 oz (50 g) unsmoked ham, thickly sliced and cut into small cubes
2 oz (50 g) cooked petits pois or garden peas
½ tablespoon wine vinegar
1 teaspoon French mustard
¼ teaspoon Worcestershire sauce
salt and freshly ground black pepper
4 tablespoons olive oil
12 black olives

Cook the pasta in plenty of boiling salted water, remembering that pasta for salads needs to be more al dente than hot pasta. Drain, refresh under cold running water, then drain again thoroughly. Pat dry with kitchen paper. Turn the pasta into a bowl, and toss immediately with the sunflower oil. Set aside until cold.

When the pasta is cold, mix in the chicken, ham and peas.

Put the vinegar, mustard, Worcestershire sauce, salt and pepper into a small bowl and add the olive oil gradually, beating with a small wire whisk or a fork, until the sauce has thickened. Check the seasoning.

Pour the sauce over the pasta mixture and toss well. Add the black olives and set aside for about 30 minutes. Serve at room temperature. Pasta salad should never be served chilled.

TAGLIATELLE RING WITH CHICKEN LIVERS

Illustrated on page 66

This is the sort of dish which would lend a touch of elegance to any dinner party. Follow it with a fresh green salad.

───────── SERVES 6 ─────────

tagliatelle made with 4 eggs and 14 oz (400 g) strong flour (page 6); or 1½ lb (675 g) shop-bought fresh tagliatelle; or 1 lb (450 g) dried egg tagliatelle
3 oz (85 g) butter
1 egg, beaten
5 fl oz (150 ml) single cream
2 tablespoons dried breadcrumbs
for the sauce
1 oz (25 g) dried porcini (wild mushrooms)
8 oz (225 g) chicken livers
2 tablespoons chopped shallot
1 oz (25 g) butter
1 tablespoon olive oil
5-6 fresh sage leaves or 4 dried sage leaves, chopped
1 tablespoon grated carrot
2 oz (50 g) lean minced beef
salt and freshly ground black pepper
1½ teaspoons tomato purée
6 tablespoons dry white vermouth
4 fl oz (110 ml) beef stock
for serving
freshly grated Parmesan cheese

To make the sauce, put the porcini into a bowl and cover with ½ pint (300 ml) warm water. Leave to soak for 30 minutes.

Meanwhile, trim the chicken livers of fat and any greenish pieces of gall. Wash them, dry thoroughly and cut into bite-size pieces.

Lift the porcini carefully from the soaking water and rinse them gently under cold running water. Dry and cut into small pieces. Strain the soaking water through a sieve lined with a piece of muslin.

Put the shallot, butter and oil into a heavy saucepan and sauté until the shallot is soft. Add the sage, sauté for 30 seconds and then mix in the carrot and the minced beef. Cook until the meat has lost its pinkness, stirring very frequently. Season to taste with salt and pepper.

Add the porcini to the pan and cook gently for a further 5 minutes. Add the chicken livers. Dissolve the tomato purée in the vermouth and pour into the pan. Raise the heat to moderate and cook for 1 minute.

Add 4 tablespoons of the strained porcini soaking liquid to the sauce with about the same amount of the stock. Cook over a low heat for 20 minutes, adding a few tablespoons more of the stock if the sauce gets too dry.

Heat the oven to 350°F (180°C, gas mark 4).

Cook the tagliatelle in plenty of boiling salted water, until still very al dente. Drain, reserving a cupful of the cooking water, then immediately turn the tagliatelle back into the saucepan in which it was cooked and add the butter. Beat the egg and cream together and add to the tagliatelle. Toss well and add 2-3 tablespoons of the reserved cooking water.

Generously butter a 1¾-pint (1-litre) ring mould and sprinkle with the breadcrumbs. Shake off the excess. Spoon the tagliatelle into the mould, pressing down gently.

Bake for 10 minutes. Turn the mould out on to a heated round serving dish and spoon the hot sauce into the centre. Serve immediately, accompanied by the Parmesan in a bowl.

Clockwise, from left: Tagliatelle Ring with Chicken Livers (page 65); Baked Tagliatelle with Mushrooms; Green Tagliatelle Mould in Creamy Cheese Sauce (page 68).

BAKED TAGLIATELLE WITH MUSHROOMS

This easy yet delicious dish can be prepared in advance, and the topping of cream, Parmesan and butter added just before you bake it. In this traditional recipe from central Italy, the porcini are not absolutely necessary, but they do approximate the taste of the wild mushrooms often used in Italy.

SERVES 6

---

tagliatelle made with 3 eggs and 11 oz (300 g) strong flour (page 6);
or 1 lb (450 g) shop-bought fresh tagliatelle; or 12 oz (340 g) dried
egg tagliatelle
1½ oz (40 g) dried porcini
2 slices white bread, crusts removed
4 fl oz (100 ml) milk
4 oz (120 g) butter
1 clove garlic, peeled and bruised
12 oz (340 g) mushrooms, cleaned and finely sliced
3 eggs, separated
salt and freshly ground black pepper
2 oz (50 g) Gruyère cheese, thinly sliced
2 oz (50 g) Bel Paese or Gouda cheese, thinly sliced
2 oz (50 g) freshly grated Parmesan cheese
5 fl oz (150 ml) double cream

Soak the porcini in a cupful of warm water for 30 minutes, then lift them out carefully. Rinse them gently under cold water, pat them dry with kitchen paper and chop them. Strain the porcini-soaking liquid through a sieve lined with kitchen paper. Reserve.

Soak the bread in the milk for about 5 minutes, then remove and squeeze out the moisture.

Heat half the butter and the garlic in a frying pan and mix in the porcini with about half the soaking liquid. Cook over moderate heat for 5 minutes, stirring frequently, until the liquid is partially evaporated. Remove and discard the garlic, add the cultivated mushrooms and season with salt and pepper. Cook over moderate heat for 5 minutes, stirring, then transfer to a bowl.

Add the egg yolks. Break up the bread with a fork and add to the mixture. Season to taste with salt and pepper and set aside.

Heat the oven to 350°F (180°C, gas mark 4).

Cook the tagliatelle in plenty of boiling salted water. Drain when still slightly undercooked and immediately toss with half the remaining butter.

Whisk the egg whites until stiff but not dry and fold into the mushroom mixture.

Butter an ovenproof dish and turn half the tagliatelle into it. Spoon over the mushroom and egg mixture and top with the sliced Gruyère and Bel Paese. Sprinkle with half the Parmesan. Cover with the remaining tagliatelle. Sprinkle over the remaining Parmesan, spoon over the cream and dot with the remaining butter.

Cover the dish with foil and bake in the oven for 15 minutes. Remove the foil, raise the heat to 425°F (220°C, gas mark 7) and bake for a further 10 minutes until brown and crusty on top. Remove from the oven and allow to stand for 5 minutes before serving, so that the flavours combine.

GREEN TAGLIATELLE MOULDS IN CREAMY CHEESE SAUCE

Illustrated on page 66

These pretty green moulds are quite delicious. If you want to make them even more appealing both to the eye and the palate, surround them with mange-tout peas, blanched until tender but still crisp and slightly crunchy.
If you have made your own tagliatelle, you will have some left over. Weigh the quantity needed to fill the ramekins and allow the remaining tagliatelle to dry very thoroughly before storing in an airtight container.

––––––––––– SERVES 4 –––––––––––

tagliatelle made with 2 eggs and 7 oz (200 g) strong flour and 5 oz (140 g) cooked spinach (page 6); or 12 oz (340 g) shop-bought fresh green tagliatelle; or 9 oz (250 g) dried tagliatelle
béchamel sauce made with ¾ oz (20 g) butter, ¾ oz (20 g) flour and ½ pint (280 ml) milk (page 76)
2 oz (50 g) freshly grated Parmesan cheese
2 oz (50 g) grated mature Cheddar cheese
freshly ground white pepper
¼ pint (150 ml) single cream
3 tablespoons dried breadcrumbs
2 oz (50 g) butter

Make the béchamel sauce as described on page 76. Blend the cheeses into the béchamel sauce and heat through very gently until they are completely melted. Season with pepper to taste. Stir the cream into the sauce and bring to simmering point (do not boil). Stir well again and check the seasoning. Turn off the heat, cover the pan and keep warm on a corner of the stove.

Heat the oven to 350°F (180°C, gas mark 4).

Butter 4×7-fl oz (200-ml) ramekins. Sprinkle with the breadcrumbs and shake off the excess.

Cook the tagliatelle in plenty of boiling salted water and drain as soon as it is very al dente. Return the tagliatelle to the saucepan in which it was cooked and immediately toss very thoroughly with the butter. Fill the ramekins with the tagliatelle and press down gently. Bake for 7 minutes.

Loosen the tagliatelle with a palette knife. Place a heated individual plate over each ramekin and turn upside down. Give a brisk shake and a tap to the top of the ramekin and lift it away.

Reheat the cheese sauce, if necessary, and pour a couple of tablespoons around each mould. Serve immediately, accompanied by the remaining sauce in a heated sauceboat or bowl.

BAKED LASAGNE WITH SEAFOOD
Illustrated on pages 70/71

This is a delicious and rich dish on which time and money should not be spared.

──────── SERVES 6 ────────

lasagne made with 2 eggs and 7 oz (300 g) strong flour (page 6); or
1 lb 2 oz (500 g) shop-bought fresh green lasagne; or 12 oz (340 g)
dried lasagne
2 small onions, very finely chopped
4 fl oz (110 ml) dry white wine
2 lb (900 g) mussels, cleaned
1 lb (450 g) squid, cleaned
1 bay leaf
salt and freshly ground black pepper
1 lb (450 g) frozen prawns in the shell, thawed
4 scallops
2 oz (50 g) butter
1½ tablespoons tomato purée
4 tablespoons dry marsala or sherry
1 tablespoon fresh or dried chilli
4 tablespoons double cream
4 tablespoons sour cream
for the sauce
½ pint (280 ml) milk
2½ oz (60 g) butter
2 oz (50 g) plain flour

Put half the onion, the wine and the mussels into a large heavy frying pan, cover and cook over a high heat until all the mussels open, shaking the pan occasionally.

Remove the mussels from the pan, reserving the cooking liquid. Remove the meat from the shells and set aside in a bowl. Discard the shells. Strain the cooking liquid through a sieve lined with muslin. Reserve.

Cut the squid tentacles into small pieces and the bodies into thin strips. Put the squid into a saucepan, add the bay leaf and some salt, and cover with water. Cook for 5-15 minutes, until the squid are tender. Remove with a slotted spoon, reserving the cooking liquid,

Remove the heads and shells from the prawns. Devein, if necessary, pat dry with kitchen paper, and add them to the bowl with the other seafood.

Put the prawn heads and shells into the squid cooking water and bring to the boil. Simmer for about 5 minutes, then strain into a bowl. Add the reserved mussel cooking liquid. Reserve.

Remove the coral from the scallops and add to the bowl with the other seafood. Slice the white scallop meat and reserve.

Heat the butter very gently with the remaining onion in the frying pan and sauté until the onion is soft. Stir in the tomato purée and sauté for 1 minute, stirring constantly. Add the marsala, chilli and about 4 tablespoons of the fish stock. Bring to the boil and simmer for 10 minutes. Remove and discard the chilli.

Mix the creams into the sauce, cook gently without boiling for 1 minute, then add the white scallop meat. Cook gently, stirring, for 1 minute.

Remove from the heat and mix in all the other seafood. Season with plenty of pepper, taste and adjust the salt.

To make the sauce, measure out ½ pint (280 ml) of the fish stock and add to the milk. Heat to just below boiling point. Melt the butter in a heavy saucepan, then blend in the flour. Cook, stirring constantly, for about 40 seconds, then remove from the heat and gradually stir in the milk and fish stock mixture. Return the pan to the heat and bring to the boil. Boil gently for 4-5 minutes, then season to taste with salt and pepper.

Heat the oven to 425°F (220°C, gas mark 7).

Meanwhile, cook and drain the lasagne as described under Baked Green Lasagne, page 72.

To assemble the dish, butter the bottom and sides of a 10×8-in (25×20-cm) ovenproof dish (preferably metal). Spread about 1 tablespoon of the sauce over the bottom. Place a layer of lasagne in the dish, cover with about 2 tablespoons of the seafood mixture and spread over a little more sauce. Cover with another layer of lasagne and repeat the layers, ending with a layer of lasagne. Spread the top with all the remaining sauce.

Bake in the oven for 25 minutes or until a golden crust has formed on top and the dish is heated through.

Remove from the oven and allow to stand for 5 minutes before serving, so that the flavours combine.

BAKED LASAGNE WITH RADICCHIO

A new recipe in which the delicate, slightly bitter flavour of the radicchio comes as an unexpected and delicious surprise.

--- SERVES 4-6 ---

lasagne made with 2 eggs and 7 oz (200 g) strong flour (page 6); or 1 lb (450 g) shop-bought fresh lasagne; or 12 oz (340 g) dry lasagne
1 lb (450 g) red radicchio
2 tablespoons olive oil
1 clove garlic, peeled and bruised
salt and freshly ground black pepper
1 pint (560 ml) béchamel sauce, flavoured with 1 bay leaf (page 76)
1 oz (25 g) butter
4 oz (120 g) freshly grated Gruyère cheese
2 oz (50 g) freshly grated Parmesan cheese
2 tablespoons dried breadcrumbs

Cut the radicchio heads in half lengthways. Remove any wilted outside leaves and part of the core. Cut each half crossways into thin strips. Wash thoroughly and drain.

Heat the oil and garlic in a large heavy frying pan until the garlic begins to colour, then remove and discard. Add the radicchio and sauté over a moderate heat for about 5 minutes. Season, then cover the pan and cook for about 20 minutes over a low heat, stirring occasionally. Check the seasoning and transfer to a bowl.

Meanwhile, make the béchamel sauce as described on page 76. Remove and discard the bay leaf. Reserve about 5 tablespoons béchamel and mix the remainder into the radicchio in the pan. Set aside.

Make the lasagne as described on page 6.

Cook and drain the lasagne as described on page 72. Heat the oven to 400°F (200°C, gas mark 6).

Grease the bottom and sides of a 10×8-in (30×20-cm) ovenproof dish (preferably metal) with some of the butter. Place a layer of lasagne over the bottom, overlapping the sheets slightly.

Spread with about 2 tablespoons of the radicchio mixture, then sprinkle with the two cheeses and a >

Left: Baked Lasagne with Radicchio, centre: Baked
Lasagne with Seafood (page 69), right: Baked Green Lasagne (page 72).

< generous grinding of pepper. Cover with another layer of lasagne, cutting the strips to fit, then a layer of the radicchio mixture, and continue to make layers in the same way, finishing with a layer of lasagne. Spread the reserved béchamel sauce over the top.

Mix any remaining grated cheese with the breadcrumbs. Sprinkle over the top of the dish and dot with the remaining butter.

Bake for about 20 minutes, until the top is light golden and crusty. Remove from the oven and leave to stand for at least 5 minutes before serving.

BAKED GREEN LASAGNE

Illustrated on pages 70/71

The recipe here is the classic version of this famous Bolognese dish. Of all pasta, lasagne is the one which is best homemade. If you cannot make your own, buy a good Italian brand of dried egg lasagne, which gives a better result than most shop-bought fresh lasagne.

―――――――――――― SERVES 4-6 ――――――――――――

lasagne made with 2 eggs and 7 oz (200 g) strong flour and 5 oz (140 g) cooked spinach (page 6); or 1 lb (450 g) shop-bought fresh green lasagne; or 12 oz (340 g) dried green lasagne
Bolognese sauce (made exactly as on page 77)
1½ pints (800 ml) béchamel sauce, flavoured with a pinch of grated nutmeg (page 76)
salt
1 tablespoon vegetable oil
1 oz (25 g) butter
2 oz (50 g) freshly grated Parmesan cheese

First make the Bolognese sauce.

While the sauce is cooking, prepare the lasagne, if you are making your own, as on page 6.

Now make the béchamel and add the nutmeg. Cover the pan with clingfilm, then a lid, and set aside.

To cook the lasagne, bring a large shallow saucepan

of water to the boil (a large deep frying pan is ideal). Add salt and the oil, which helps to prevent the lasagne from sticking to each other. When the water is boiling fast, drop in about 6 lasagne, one at a time, and stir with a wooden spoon. Place a large bowl of cold water near the pan and lay clean tea towels on a work surface.

When the lasagne is cooked, lift each sheet out with a fish slice and plunge into the cold water, then transfer to the tea towel. Pat dry with kitchen paper. Cook and drain all the lasagne in the same way.

Heat the oven to 425°F (220°C, gas mark 7).

Grease a 12×8-in (30×20-cm) ovenproof rectangular dish (preferably metal), with half the butter. Spread about 2 tablespoons of the Bolognese sauce over the bottom of the dish and cover with a layer of lasagne sheets; do not overlap them too much. Spread over another couple of tablespoons of the Bolognese sauce and some béchamel. Sprinkle with Parmesan. Cover with another layer of lasagne, Bolognese and béchamel sauces and repeat the layers until all the ingredients are used up, finishing with a layer of béchamel. Sprinkle with the remaining cheese.

Melt the remaining butter and pour over the dish. Bake in the oven for 20 minutes until the top is lightly crusty. Remove from the oven and leave to stand for 5 minutes before serving.

AUBERGINE AND MACARONI CAKE
Illustrated on page 75

*This is a very showy south Italian dish.
It can be prepared a few hours in advance.*

———————— SERVES 6 ————————

14 oz (400 g) rigatoni
2 aubergines, total weight about 1 lb (450 g)
salt and freshly ground black pepper
double quantity plain tomato sauce (page 77)
vegetable oil for frying
3 oz (85 g) butter
1 Italian mozzarella cheese, coarsely grated or chopped
4 tablespoons freshly grated Parmesan cheese
4 tablespoons grated mature Cheddar cheese
1 tablespoon oregano
2 tablespoons dried breadcrumbs

Peel the aubergines and cut them into ¼-in (6-mm) slices. Place a board on the slant over the sink. Put layers of aubergine slices over the board, sprinkling each layer with salt. Leave to drain for 1 hour. Rinse thoroughly and pat each slice dry. Make the tomato sauce as described on page 77.

Heat enough frying oil in a large frying pan to come about 1 in (2.5 cm) up the sides of the pan. When a corner of an aubergine slice dipped into it sizzles, the oil is hot enough. Slide in a few slices of aubergine at a time and fry until deep golden on both sides. Do not overcrowd the slices or they will not fry properly.

Remove the fried aubergines with a slotted spoon, drain well and place in a dish lined with kitchen paper.

Cook the macaroni in plenty of salted boiling water until still slightly undercooked. Drain and return the macaroni to the saucepan in which it was cooked and toss with 2 tablespoons of the tomato sauce.

Add the butter to the remaining tomato sauce in a saucepan and heat gently until the butter is melted. Pour over the macaroni and toss. Mix in the 3 cheeses, the pepper and oregano. Check the seasoning.

Heat the oven to 375°F (190°C, gas mark 5).

Line the base of an 8-in (20-cm) spring-form tin with aubergine slices. Fill in any gaps with pieces of aubergine. Line the sides of the tin with aubergine slices, cutting to fit. Place any aubergine left over in the bottom of the tin. Fill the tin with the macaroni mixture and press down lightly. Sprinkle with the breadcrumbs.

Bake for 20 minutes or until the filling is hot.

Remove from the oven and run a palette knife around the side of the tin. Place a heated round serving dish over the top of the tin and invert the tin. Tap the base of the tin and give the dish a sharp shake or two. Unclip the ring and lift the tin away carefully. If necessary, press into place any pieces of aubergine stuck to the tin. Allow the cake to stand for the flavours to combine.

CANNELLONI WITH PORK, VEAL AND CHICKEN
Illustrated on page 75

These cannelloni are delicate, yet full of flavour. Both the cannelloni and sauces can be made ahead.

———————— MAKES 20 CANNELLONI ————————

lasagne made with 1 egg and 3½ oz (100 g) strong flour (page 6); or
10 shop-bought fresh lasagne; or 10 dried lasagne
Tomato Sauce (page 77)
Béchamel Sauce (page 76)
2 oz (50 g) butter
4 oz (120 g) lean pork fillet, cut into small cubes
4 oz (120 g) lean pie veal, cut into small cubes
4 oz (120 g) boneless chicken breast, cut into small cubes
3 oz (85 g) mortadella or prosciutto, cut into small pieces
1 large egg, beaten
3 tablespoons freshly grated Parmesan cheese
pinch of grated nutmeg
salt and freshly ground black pepper
butter for greasing

Cook the lasagne as described on page 6. Lay the >

< cooked lasagne on a clean tea towel while you prepare the sauces and stuffing.

Make the tomato sauce as described on page 77. Meanwhile, prepare the béchamel sauce as described on page 76. Cover the béchamel with clingfilm to prevent a skin from forming, then cover with a lid.

To make the stuffing, melt the butter in a heavy frying pan and as soon as it begins to foam, add the pork and sauté over a moderate heat for 5 minutes.

Reduce the heat to low and add the veal and the chicken. Fry gently, turning, for about 2 minutes, until the meat is white. Transfer to a chopping board. Add the mortadella and chop finely, or process in a food processor for just a few seconds: do not blend to a paste; the mixture should be coarse. Transfer the mixture to a bowl and mix in the egg, cheese, nutmeg and salt and pepper to taste.

Heat the oven to 400°F (200°C, gas mark 6).

Grease an ovenproof dish, preferably metal and rectangular, large enough to hold the cannelloni in a single layer. If using bought lasagne, cut each sheet in half.

Lay a sheet of lasagne on a board and spread about 1 heaped tablespoon of stuffing over it, leaving a ½-inch (1-cm) border all round the edge. Roll the lasagne up loosely from one short end. Lay it in the dish, seam side down. Continue in this way until all the stuffing mixture is used up.

Spread the tomato sauce over the cannelloni. Spread the béchamel over it and, with a spatula, swirl the sauces so that some of the tomato sauce will show through.

Bake for about 20 minutes. Remove from the oven and leave to stand for about 5 minutes, to allow all the flavours to combine, then serve.

CANNELLONI IN WALNUT AND HORSERADISH SAUCE

The filling for these cannelloni is very delicate. They can be dressed with a thin béchamel sauce (page 76) or with the cream and butter sauce with the recipe for Fettuccine on page 21. But I think the walnut sauce given here goes best with them because its particular taste blends beautifully with that of the filling, while it provides an interesting contrast in texture. This dish is ideal for vegetarians.

—————— **MAKES 20 CANNELLONI** ——————

lasagne made with 1 large egg and 3½ oz (100 g) strong flour (page 6); or 10 shop-bought fresh lasagne; or 10 dried lasagne
1 pint (560 ml) béchamel sauce (page 76)
1 lb (450 g) ricotta cheese
freshly grated nutmeg
3 tablespoons chopped coriander leaves
3 tablespoons chopped parsley
4 tablespoons freshly grated Parmesan cheese
freshly ground black pepper
butter for greasing
for the walnut sauce
1 oz (25 g) white bread, crusts removed
a little milk
4 oz (120 g) shelled walnuts
2 tablespoons olive oil
¾ pint (450 ml) single cream
2 teaspoons grated horseradish
3 tablespoons freshly grated Parmesan cheese
salt and freshly ground black pepper

To make the sauce, soak the bread in the milk for 5 minutes. Put the bread with the milk in a blender or food processor and add the walnuts. Process for 5 seconds, scrape down the sides of the goblet and process again for a further 5 seconds, until the mixture is coarse and grainy.

Transfer the mixture to a bowl. Gradually beat in >

Clockwise, from left: Aubergine and Macaroni Cake (page 73); Cannelloni with Pork, Veal and Chicken (page 73); Cannelloni in Walnut and Horseradish Sauce.

< the oil and cream, then add the horseradish, Parmesan and salt and pepper to taste. Set aside.

Make the béchamel sauce as described on this page.

Pass the ricotta through a food mill or a metal sieve into a bowl. Blend in the béchamel sauce and stir well to blend thoroughly. Add the nutmeg, coriander, parsley, Parmesan and pepper. Check the seasoning and add salt, if necessary.

Heat the oven to 400°F (200°C, gas mark 6).

Cook the lasagne as described under Baked Green Lasagne, page 72. If using bought lasagne, cut them in half.

Spread about 1 tablespoon of the filling over the middle of each lasagne sheet, roll it up from a short end and lay seam side down in a greased ovenproof dish large enough to hold all the cannelloni in a single layer.

Spoon the walnut sauce over the cannelloni, cover with foil and bake for 20 minutes. Remove from the oven and leave to stand for 4-5 minutes before serving.

BECHAMEL SAUCE

Pasta was happily married to this sauce long before the Marquis de Béchamel, steward to Louis XIV, gave it its name. The sauce is essential in many baked pasta dishes and you can flavour it by infusing the milk with a bay leaf, a clove of garlic, or a slice of onion instead of using the more popular nutmeg. It can be made thicker or thinner by using less or more milk.

—————— **MAKES 1 PINT (560 ML)** ——————

1 pint (560 ml) milk
2 oz (50 g) butter
1½ oz (40 g) plain flour
a pinch of grated nutmeg
salt and freshly ground black pepper

Bring the milk to simmering point.

Meanwhile, melt the butter in a heavy saucepan over a low heat and blend in the flour, using a wooden spoon. Cook, stirring constantly, for 30 seconds.

Remove the pan from the heat and gradually add the hot milk to the butter and flour mixture, beating constantly.

When the sauce is thoroughly blended and smooth, return the pan to the heat. Return very slowly to the boil, then simmer very gently, stirring frequently for 20 minutes, to allow the flour to cook thoroughly. Season with the nutmeg and salt and pepper to taste.

BOLOGNESE SAUCE

Called ragù in Italian, this is the main sauce for baked lasagne. It is also perfect with tagliatelle or macaroni. There are numerous versions: the one I give here is a classic. The important thing to remember is that a good ragù needs to be cooked, at the lowest simmer, for at least 2 hours. Ragù can be kept in the refrigerator for up to 5 days, or it can be frozen. Thaw, reheat and simmer for 15 minutes before using.

SERVES 4

3 tablespoons olive oil
1 oz (25 g) butter
4 oz (120 g) pancetta or unsmoked streaky bacon, rinded and diced
1 small onion, very finely chopped
1 small carrot, very finely chopped
1 stalk celery, very finely chopped
1 small clove garlic, peeled and crushed
12 oz (340 g) best minced beef
2 oz (50 g) chicken livers, trimmed and chopped
4 fl oz (110 ml) dry white wine
2 tablespoons tomato purée
4 fl oz (110 ml) beef stock
salt and freshly ground black pepper
4 tablespoons single cream

Put the oil, butter, pancetta, onion, carrot and celery into a heavy saucepan and cook over a moderate heat, stirring from time to time, until the vegetables are soft. Add the garlic, beef and chicken livers and sauté until the beef has lost its pinkness.

Pour in the wine and boil briskly until reduced by more than half. Mix the tomato purée with the stock and add to the pan. Check the seasoning and bring to the boil. Mix well and simmer very gently, uncovered, for 2-2½ hours, stirring occasionally. The sauce should on no account boil, but just break into an occasional bubble. If the sauce gets too dry, add a little warm water.

15 minutes before the ragù is ready, stir in the cream and check the seasoning.

PLAIN TOMATO SAUCE

This simple tomato sauce can be used as a base for many other sauces. It is also very good on its own as a dressing for pasta, with some butter or oil added just before serving, for extra richness. The sauce keeps very well in the refrigerator for up to 4 days and may also be frozen.

14 oz (400 g) tinned plum tomatoes
½ small onion, halved
1 stalk celery, chopped
½ small carrot, thickly sliced into rounds
1 bay leaf
1 teaspoon tomato purée
½ teaspoon sugar
salt and freshly ground black pepper

Put all the ingredients into a small saucepan and bring to the boil. Cook uncovered at a steady simmer for 30 minutes or until the sauce is thick. If it becomes too dry add a couple of tablespoons of hot water.

Remove and discard the bay leaf, then purée the sauce in a food mill or through a sieve.

GLOSSARY OF INGREDIENTS

Mozzarella This low-fat cheese is still made traditionally in the south of Italy from the milk of water buffalos, but outside Italy it is made from cow's milk. It can be rather tasteless and slightly rubbery, but its main use is as a binding agent. After unwrapping, mozzarella can be kept in the refrigerator for up to 8 days in a bowl with its whey, and covered with cold salted water. The water should be changed every day. Unwrapped mozzarella can be frozen.

Parmesan This is a very hard cheese which has aged for at least a year, and sometimes for up to three years. It is the perfect accompaniment to most pasta dishes, but should certainly not be sprinkled regardless on every dish. I have only included it in the list of ingredients when it is an essential part of the dish.

Parmesan should be crumbly in texture, buff-yellow in colour and mellow, rich and slightly salty in taste. When you come across Parmesan in this ideal condition, buy a large piece, cut it into ½-lb (225-g) wedges and wrap each one in a double thickness of foil. Keep one or two pieces in the refrigerator and freeze the remainder. Parmesan should always be freshly grated, as its flavour fades very quickly. Try and avoid commercial ready-grated Parmesan if you can.

Pecorino romano This is a cheese made from ewe's milk, and has a pungent, salty but very pleasant taste when fresh. Unfortunately it acquires an unpleasant, sickly taste with age, so always ask to taste it before you buy it, and if you cannot get good pecorino, use Parmesan instead.

Ricotta This is a very soft white cheese made from the whey of other cheeses and though very low in fat, has a bland creamy taste. It is highly perishable and only keeps for 48 hours at most. Taste ricotta before you buy it, to make sure it does not have an acid, bitter taste.

Luganega or salsiccia a metro This is a mild, coarse-grained Italian pork sausage for which there is really no substitute. It is now available in vacuum packs in many supermarkets or loose in Italian or specialist delicatessens.

Pancetta This is cured and spiced belly of pork, either rolled up into a salami shape (pancetta arrotolata), or cut straight like bacon (pancetta stesa). The latter is the best for cooking and is sold in Italian shops and specialist delicatessens. Pancetta freezes very well; I buy it in large quantities, then divide it into 3½ oz (100 g) packets and freeze them. Mild unsmoked streaky bacon is a good substitute, although for the authentic Italian flavour you need the real thing.

Dried porcini or funghi secchi These dried wild mushrooms, sold in ⅓-oz (10-g) or ¾-oz (20-g) sachets are available from many supermarkets or specialist shops. They are expensive, but as little as ⅓ oz (10 g) makes a considerable difference to the finished dish, especially when used in combination with cultivated mushrooms. When you buy porcini, check the packet to make sure they are in large pieces, not small crumbly bits.

Tomatoes Fresh tomatoes are rarely good enough to give the necessary flavour to sauces, unless you grow them yourself or buy imported plum or Marmande tomatoes, at the height of the season. Otherwise, buy Italian tinned tomatoes, preferably San Marzano, which are sweet and do not have that slightly metallic, acid taste that you may find in other kinds.

Pepper Use peppercorns which you can grind yourself, rather than ready-ground pepper. Black pepper is more aromatic, yet less pungent, than white pepper, and is to be preferred. When I suggest white pepper, this is simply for appearance's sake: if a sauce is white or creamy, black pepper would give it an unattractive speckled appearance. Add pepper towards the end of the cooking, because it loses its aroma if cooked for too long. Do not add too much pepper to sauces containing delicately-flavoured ingredients.

Olive oil This has a low cholesterol content, and is the only oil that is made without the use of any chemicals in its manufacture. In almost every recipe in this book where oil is used, olive oil is essential for the flavour of the sauce. Rich, green olive oil, tasting of the fruit, is infinitely superior to the over-refined type. In some recipes I have listed extra virgin olive oil, which is the oil that comes from the first pressing of the olives and its acidity is minimal — less than 1 per cent.

INDEX